Celebrate
Wool Appliqué

Deborah Gale Tirico

30 FOLK ART PROJECTS

7 Gift Sets

C&T PUBLISHING

Text, photography, and artwork copyright © 2019 by Deborah Gale Tirico

Photography and artwork copyright © 2019 by C&T Publishing, Inc.

Publisher: Amy Marson

Creative Director: Gailen Runge

Acquisitions Editor: Roxane Cerda

Managing Editor: Liz Aneloski

Editor: Karla Menaugh

Technical Editor: Helen Frost

Cover/Book Designer: April Mostek

Production Coordinator: Zinnia Heinzmann

Production Editor: Alice Mace Nakanishi

Illustrators: Deborah Gale Tirico and Kirstie L. Pettersen

Photo Assistants: Rachel Holmes and Mai Yong Vang

Cover photography by Lucy Glover of C&T Publishing, Inc.

Instructional photography by Deborah Gale Tirico; style photography by Kelly Burgoyne and Lucy Glover and subject photography by Mai Yong Vang of C&T Publishing, Inc., unless otherwise noted

Published by C&T Publishing, Inc., P.O. Box 1456, Lafayette, CA 94549

Library of Congress Cataloging-in-Publication Data

Names: Tirico, Deborah Gale, 1953- author.

Title: Celebrate wool appliqué : 30 folk art projects 7 gift sets / Deborah Gale Tirico.

Description: Lafayette, CA : C&T Publishing, Inc., [2019]

Identifiers: LCCN 2018033605 | ISBN 9781617457753 (softcover)

Subjects: LCSH: Appliqué--Patterns. | Wool quilts. | Folk art--United States.

Classification: LCC TT779 .T579 2019 | DDC 746.44/5--dc23

LC record available at https://lccn.loc.gov/2018033605

Printed in China

10 9 8 7 6 5 4 3 2 1

Dedication

To my friend Helene—my stitching buddy, roomie, homie, and pal. Thanks for all the *oohs* and *aahs* to everything I have ever made. Your company on long road trips, consistent support of my creative work, and your friendship is a treasure. Thank you, H!

Acknowledgments

To my son, Frankie, who helps me realize my dreams by taking videos, carrying bolts of wool to the studio, photographing my work, and paying attention—thank you, my son.

To my husband, Frank, who dyes wool fabric, helps me with color consultation, packs my car, cooks for me, and loves me through all the ups and downs of this crazy business—thank you, my dear.

To my mom, who appreciates my work more than anyone I know and has done so since I was a child. Thanks, Mommy!

Contents

LET'S GET SEWING

Foreword

My sister can do anything! She became an accomplished ballerina, re-created Civil War clothing and accessories, ran a successful advertising agency, gracefully twirled through ballroom dancing, learned to play classical guitar, and designed and stitched gorgeous quilts and wallhangings. Through the years, she was driven to perfect one thing that incorporates her artistic flair and stitching talents. It's now reflected in the true art I see in her wool appliqué designs.

Deb has always been a creative person. She puts her heart into her creations, enabling us to appreciate her talents and artist's touch in appliqué. I am both enamored and envious of the ease with which she creates beautiful art from wool and thread.

In this new book, she shares some of her most creative decorative accessories. Her delicate stitches have brought out the beauty of the felted wool colors and the uniqueness of these designs will inspire you. Every stitch contributes to a beautiful creation that can be display with pride. Deb has created accessories to hold tools for stitching, as well as covered boxes, coasters, wedding banners, and table decor.

Enjoy leafing through this compilation of items and choose the one which you might bring to life and reinforce your love of stitching.

Find delight in every stitch as you explore your own creative talent in the world of appliqué.

Cynthia Arruda
Moorestown, New Jersey

Introduction

Appliqué is fun—this is my mantra.

For those who absolutely love to hold a needle and thread and have a romance with wool appliqué, this book is for you. If you love to choose thread colors, buy fabrics because they speak to you, and get more excitement giving a handmade wool item than making it, I assembled these projects for you.

Sewing accessories, covered boxes, and sweet candle mats are among the many projects in this book to appoint your home or gift to a friend. Also, many of the designs can be translated into different applications. For example, the *Feathered Friends* Table Mat (page 32) can be reduced and stitched for the top of a sewing box. Use your own color sense to make these designs bright and electric or soft and muted, depending on what colors appeal to you. Some of the projects are perfect for using scraps from your stash.

For each project, there is an indication for level of experience from beginner to advanced. In many cases, the directions include strategies for stitching progressions to improved accuracy. Every word is deliberately focused on making the projects fun and the maker successful.

In Refresh Me (page 88), you will find content on the techniques I use in condensed versions to refresh you on the processes outlined in my first two books.

Finishing (page 84) provides general instructions on how to complete your stitched appliqué to cover a box, as well as how to make twisted cord and how to finish a candle mat.

Have fun and make the projects your own. Choose colors, threads, and embellishments that appeal to you and stitch the designs you like on the applications you want. Experiment!

Happy stitching!

—Deborah Gale Tirico

How to Use This Book

Stitching Glossary

At the end of the book is the illustrated Stitching Glossary (page 95). Please refer to it often. When I design, I often have a reference on embroidery stitches open to guide me in beginning a stitch that is in my memory but that I have not used lately. The projects do not include instructions on embroidery stitches, as I figure you can just flip to the glossary whenever you need some help.

Full-Size Placement Guides

You will find full-size placement guides at the ends of the chapters or on pullout pages P1 and P2. These guides serve two functions: You can trace them onto acetate or vinyl to use as a placement guide for appliqué pieces and use them as an embroidery key for which stitches and embellishments to use. (Note that the full-size placement guide is not to be used for the pattern piece creation.)

Pattern Piece Pages

Patterns for the appliqué pieces follow each project. Use these when making freezer-paper appliqué pieces. These patterns differ significantly from the pieces depicted on the full-size patterns because they include pieces that overlap and stack. If you use adhesive bond techniques, you need to reverse the patterns.

Felted Wool Appliqué Mantras

As an instructor as well as an author, I have a few mantras that I frequently use when I work. Adopt these maxims as your own and you will be rewarded with beautiful felted wool appliqué.

EMBRACE THE BASTE

Basting is the most important part of appliqué. If you want accuracy in your design, you need to hold the pieces in place, as wool can shift quite easily in the warm hands of its maker.

If you are someone who likes to skip basting or who considers it a pesky task that prevents you from getting right to the stitching part, I encourage you to learn to enjoy doing it.

Throughout the book are many illustrations that demonstrate basting techniques. Although this may be a temporary stitch, it will be your most important stitch. So, embrace the baste!

USE A FEATHERLIGHT TOUCH

Use a "light" hand and a stab stitch motion to appliqué wool. With the stab stitch, stitches will be accurately placed, and you can carefully work around any frays.

Pull your thread gently until a small loop is left and slowly complete the stitch, allowing the thread to rest gently on the side of the appliqué pieces. Never pull tightly! Pulling the thread tightly will bunch up the work and make it less attractive. Often it is better to pull that extra last bit on the next needle up, as the thread will have more drag and thus more control.

FOLLOW THE PLACEMENT GUIDE

When the project instructions direct you to place appliqué pieces according to the placement guide, don't try to eyeball it for the sake of speed. If you don't plan to position the next pieces of your appliqué using a clear placement guide hinged to the top of your project, you will likely regret the shortcut. Use the full-size placement guides for accurate placement. They are hinged to the base fabric with straight pins which allows you to flip the guide up and down to position your pieces underneath and in their proper places.

Tesoros:
Mastering the Colonial Knot

Skill level: Confident beginner/intermediate

Tesoros means "treasure" in Spanish and a treasure box filled with accessories for sewing tools is a gold mine for the needle worker. The beautiful circular box features an appliquéd top and sides and is completely covered and lined in luscious felted wool. Inside the box are complementing accessories including a needlebook, pincushion, and a scissors sheath and fob. Inspired by the colorful designs of Mexico, this design was created after seeing a plethora of Mexican artwork in the shops and galleries of San Antonio, Texas.

The design features the colonial knot which, once learned, is a beautiful, round, easy-to-stitch knot. This project, which features many colonial knots, will ensure this knot becomes part of the maker's proficient stitches.

SUPPLIES

These supplies are for the entire gift set.

- Black felted wool for base and backing, 21″ × 32″

- Weeks Dye Works wool (*or* other wool fabric in similar colors):
  Blue Topaz (bright blue), ½ yard
  Chartreuse (bright yellow-green), 8″ × 9″
  Purple Rain (bright purple), 7″ × 7″
  Candy Apple (bright red), 6″ × 6″
  Lemon Chiffon (bright yellow), 3″ × 3″
  Pumpkin (orange), 3″ × 3″

- Weeks Dye Works wool thread:
  Banana Popsicle (yellow)
  Chartreuse (bright yellow-green)
  Turquoise
  Pumpkin (orange)
  Bubble Gum (bright pink)
  Mascara (black)

- Vineyard wool thread in Fern (bright green)

- Bella Lusso wool thread in Blueberry 229 (blue) and Tomato 764 (red)

- Perle cotton #5 and #8 in black

- Milliners, chenille, and embroidery needles

- Paper punch

- Papier-mâché box, 10″ diameter

- Elmer's School Glue

- 1″ paintbrush

- White and black quilting thread

- Polyester batting

- Mini drill for making twisted cord

- Tart tin, 3½″ diameter

- Polyester craft stuffing

- Glue gun and glue sticks

Appliquéd Covered Sewing Box

Finished size: 10″ diameter

Prework

Refer to the placement guide pattern (pullout page P1) and to Refresh Me (page 88) for detailed instructions.

1. Create a clear vinyl placement guide.

2. Create a tissue-paper embroidery guide.

3. Prepare the base fabric, adding a stitched line as a guide for the live area for appliqué and to help you accurately position the top piece when constructing the box.

Construction

Refer to Refresh Me (page 88) for detailed instructions on freezer-paper patterns and the slanted-needle technique. Refer to Stitching Glossary (page 95) for an illustration of each stitch.

STEP ONE: BEGIN THE EMBROIDERY

1. Position the embroidery guide and pin in place. Stitch the embroidery guide, using Chartreuse sewing thread.

2. Embroider the spiral stems, using 2 lengths of Chartreuse wool thread. Chainstitch the spirals over the stitches made with the embroidery guide.

Note

It's important to stitch the spiral stems before you place the wool appliqué shapes. Once the spirals are stitched, you can place the other shapes accurately.

STEP TWO: PREPARING FOR APPLIQUÉ

1. Referring to the patterns (page 18), use freezer-paper methods to create the wool appliqué shapes. Wait to create the small circles until you are ready to embroider them to the base.

2. Line up and hinge the placement guide on top of the felted wool base, securing with straight pins along the top edge.

3. Place the appliqué shapes in position and pin.

4. Baste all shapes, using white cotton thread and a milliners needle.

STEP THREE: APPLIQUÉ

1. Appliqué the pieces with matching wool thread and a chenille needle, using the slanted-needle technique.

2. When stitching the flowers and buds, it is important to get them straight. Follow the stitching diagram and stitch the valleys and petal centers first to make certain the flower is straight. Fill in the balance of the appliqué stitches afterward.

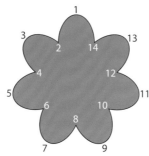

Stitching diagram

- -

tip *Thread all your wool thread colors on separate needles so you can toggle between colors as you work on these tiny areas.*

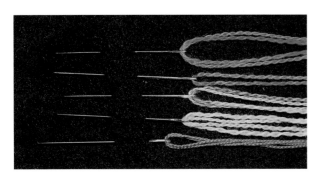

- -

3. Use a light hand and never pull your stitches tight. Rather, allow them to rest gently on the side of the appliqué piece. If you want to tighten the stitch slightly, do this after drawing the needle up to the front once again so there is more drag and therefore more control.

STEP FOUR: EMBROIDERY

Leaves

Embellish the leaves with embroidery, using Vineyard wool thread in Fern or similar bright green thread. Begin with the stem stitch down the center of the leaf. Straightstitch the side veins as outlined in the stitch detail below.

Beginning at the base of the center vein, stitch up and then down at a slant, creating the veins on the right side on the way up, and the veins on the left side on the way down. Follow the arrows on the illustration to make these veins accurate.

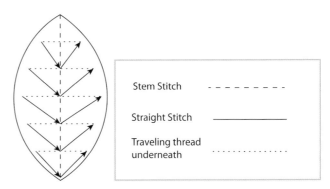

Stem Stitch	- - - - - - - -
Straight Stitch	————
Traveling thread underneath	···········

Circles and Knots

1. Using a paper punch, create small circles of color as follows:

- Lemon Chiffon for the spiral buds (Cut 18.)
- Blue Topaz for the flower centers (Cut 4.)
- Candy Apple for the bud centers (Cut 7.)
- Pumpkin for the bud centers (Cut 2.)

The paper-punch method does not cut all the way through on at least one side, so use sharp embroidery scissors to cut the rest of the circle from the fabric. The threads will be weakened from the punch and it should be easy to see where to cut.

2. Using a double length of turquoise wool thread, stitch elongated lazy daisy stitches inside the Purple Rain flowers and buds. Add a straight stitch to fill the middle of the lazy daisy. I use a stab stitch motion to get these stitches to lie correctly.

3. Using the same thread and with a single colonial knot, affix the Candy Apple circles to the base circles on the Purple Rain buds on the lid and side. Affix the Pumpkin circles to the base circles on the Candy Apple buds on the side. Do the same for the Lemon Chiffon circles on each spiral stem on the lid and side. Add colonial knots to each petal edge on the Candy Apple flowers and buds on the lid and side.

4. Using banana Popsicle wool thread, stitch elongated lazy daisy stitches and straight stitches inside the Candy Apple flowers on the lid and the Candy Apple buds on the side.

5. Using a double length of Bubble Gum wool thread, add colonial knots to the petals on the Purple Rain flowers and buds on the lid and side. Add colonial knots to each petal edge on the Purple Rain flowers and buds on the lid and side. Add colonial knots to the spiral stems of the Candy Apple buds on the side.

6. Using a double length of Pumpkin wool thread and with a single colonial knot, affix the Candy Apple circles to the Purple Rain flowers and buds on the lid and side. Affix the Blue Topaz circles to the Candy Apple flowers on the lid. Add colonial knots to the spiral stems on the Purple Rain flowers and buds on the lid and side.

7. Using a single length of Mascara wool thread, add straight stitches between the petals on the flowers and buds to delineate the petals.

8. Make lazy daisy flowers on each side with Bubble Gum thread and a colonial knot for the center with turquoise thread.

STEP FIVE: FINISH THE BOX

Refer to Making Covered Boxes (page 84) for detailed instructions on finishing the box.

Needlebook

Finished size: 3″ × 4½″

Prework

Refer to the placement guide pattern (pullout page P1) and to Refresh Me (page 88) for detailed instructions.

1. Create a clear vinyl placement guide.

2. Prepare the base fabric.

3. Create an embroidery guide.

Construction

Refer to Refresh Me (page 88) for detailed instructions on freezer-paper patterns and the slanted-needle technique. Refer to Stitching Glossary (page 95) for an illustration of each stitch.

STEP ONE: PREPARING FOR APPLIQUÉ

1. Referring to the patterns (page 18), use freezer-paper methods to create the wool appliqué shapes.

Using rotary cutting methods, cut:

• Chartreuse felted wool: 3″ × 4½″

• Topaz blue felted wool: 4½″ × 6″

• Bubble gum felted wool: 3″ × 4½″

2. Line up and hinge the placement guide at the top of the felted wool base, securing with straight pins along the top edge.

3. Place and pin the appliqué shapes in position.

4. Baste all shapes, using white cotton thread and a milliners needle.

Circles

Using a paper punch, create small circles of color as follows:

- Lemon Chiffon for the spiral buds (Cut 2.)
- Candy Apple for the flower and bud centers (Cut 2.)

STEPS TWO AND THREE: APPLIQUÉ AND EMBROIDERY

1. Using matching wool thread, appliqué the shapes in place on the front of the needle book. For dimension in your appliqué, use the slanted-needle technique.

2. Follow the placement guide and the embroidery instructions for the previous *Tesoros* project to complete the embroidery embellishment.

STEP FOUR: ASSEMBLY

1. Position the Chartreuse green lining on the inside front, and the Bubble Gum lining piece on the inside back, lining them up with the top and sides of the book. There will be space between them for the spine. Using a length of black perle cotton #8, blanket stitch the outer edges, leaving the inside edges open to be used as a pockets.

2. Position the Blue Topaz wool piece on top of the entire open assembly and secure the center with a running stitch in black perle cotton #8.

3. Secure the needlebook, using a tiny red button and a blanket-stitched loop in turquoise wool thread.

Add some needles to the book and it's done—a soft and easy-to-use needlebook for you or a stitching friend.

Pincushion

Finished size: 3½″ diameter

Prework

Refer to the placement guide pattern (page 19) and to Refresh Me (page 88) for detailed instructions.

1. Create a clear vinyl placement guide.

2. Prepare the base fabric.

Construction

Refer to Refresh Me (page 88) for detailed instructions on freezer-paper patterns and the slanted-needle technique.
Refer to Stitching Glossary (page 95) for an illustration of each stitch.

STEP ONE: PREPARING FOR APPLIQUÉ

1. Referring to the patterns (page 19), use freezer-paper methods to create the wool appliqué shapes.

2. Pin and baste the appliqué pieces in position as described in previous *Tesoros* projects.

Circles

Using a paper punch, create small circles of color as follows:

• Candy Apple for the bud centers (Cut 4.)

STEPS TWO AND THREE: APPLIQUÉ AND EMBROIDERY

Appliqué and embellish the pincushion design as described in previous *Tesoros* projects.

STEP FOUR: ASSEMBLY

1. Cut out the circle along the white line and, using a milliners needle and a double length of white quilting thread, stitch a running stitch along the circumference ¼″ in from the edge.

2. Place a good-sized ball of stuffing inside and gather the base into a ball. Once you are pleased with the amount of stuffing, secure the quilting thread and tie off tightly by running extra stitches through again a few times and securing with a knot.

3. Using a glue gun, place a healthy amount of glue on the inside edges and bottom of the tart tin and place the pincushion inside. Work quickly so the glue doesn't begin to set before you have the cushion inside.

Add a few pins and voila!

Scissors Sheath and Fob

Finished sheath: 3½″ × 8″ • **Finished fob:** 2⅛″ diameter

Prework

Refer to the placement guide pattern (pullout page P1) and to Refresh Me (page 88) for detailed instructions.

1. Create a clear vinyl placement guide.

2. Create a tissue-paper embroidery guide.

3. Prepare the base fabric.

Construction

Refer to Refresh Me (page 88) for detailed instructions on freezer-paper patterns and the slanted-needle technique. Refer to Stitching Glossary (page 95) for an illustration of each stitch.

STEP ONE: PREPARING FOR APPLIQUÉ

1. Referring to the patterns (page 20), use freezer-paper methods to create the wool appliqué shapes.

Note: The lining pieces for the front and back are slightly smaller than the exterior pieces, so be careful to use the appropriate pattern for all 4 pieces.

Use a paper punch to create small circles of color as follows:

• Lemon Chiffon for the spiral buds (Cut 4.)

• Pumpkin for the bud center (Cut 1.)

• Blue Topaz for the flower centers (Cut 2.)

• Candy Apple for the flower and bud centers (Cut 3.)

2. Pin and baste the appliqué pieces in position as described in the *Tesoros* Needlebook project (page 14).

STEPS TWO AND THREE: APPLIQUÉ AND EMBROIDERY

Appliqué and embellish the sheath and fob designs, using the same methods as in the previous *Tesoros* projects.

STEP FOUR: MAKING THE SHEATH

1. Position the front, Bubble Gum pink lining, Chartreuse lining, and back in a sandwich and baste together, using white cotton thread.

2. Using black perle cotton #8, blanket stitch the edges, securing the corners with 3 or 4 stitches to secure the stress areas.

STEP FIVE: MAKING THE FOB

1. Make the twisted cord, using 6 lengths of perle cotton #5 in 36″ lengths. See Making Twisted Cord (page 87) for detailed instructions.

2. Place the appliquéd fob pieces together, wrong sides facing, and put the 2 ends of the twisted cord inside. Using black perle cotton #8, blanket stitch the edges, catching and securing the twisted cord inside.

Secure the fob to your scissors handle with a slip knot and tuck your scissors inside their new home!

Tesoros Appliquéd Covered Sewing Box

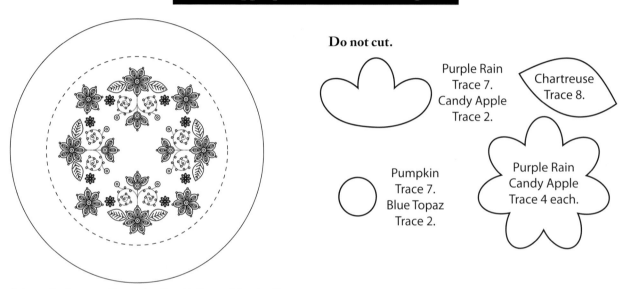

Do not cut.

Purple Rain Trace 7. Candy Apple Trace 2.

Chartreuse Trace 8.

Pumpkin Trace 7. Blue Topaz Trace 2.

Purple Rain Candy Apple Trace 4 each.

Schematic diagram: *Tesoros* Appliquéd Covered Sewing Box—top

Schematic diagram: *Tesoros* Appliquéd Covered Sewing Box—side

Tesoros Needlebook

Schematic diagram: *Tesoros* Needlebook

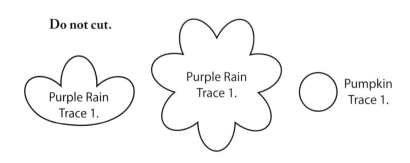

Do not cut.

Purple Rain Trace 1.

Purple Rain Trace 1.

Pumpkin Trace 1.

Tesoros Pincushion

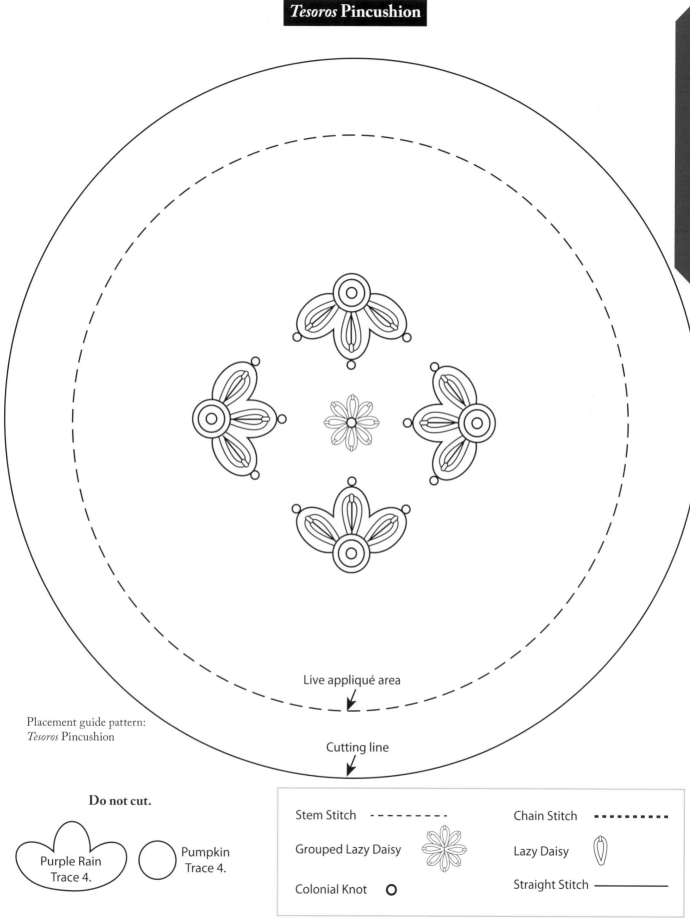

Live appliqué area

Cutting line

Placement guide pattern:
Tesoros Pincushion

Do not cut.

Purple Rain
Trace 4.

Pumpkin
Trace 4.

Stem Stitch	- - - - - - -	Chain Stitch	••••••••••••
Grouped Lazy Daisy		Lazy Daisy	
Colonial Knot	⭕	Straight Stitch	————

Tesoros Scissors Sheath and Fob

Schematic diagram:
Tesoros Scissors Fob

Schematic diagram:
Tesoros Scissors Sheath—front

Schematic diagram:
Tesoros Scissors Sheath—back

Do not cut.

Blue Topaz
Candy Apple
Trace 1 each.

Purple Rain
Candy Apple
Trace 1 each.

Purple Rain
Candy Apple
Trace 2 each.

Lining front only
Purple Rain
Trace 1.

Lining back only
Chartreuse
Trace 1.

Tesoritos:
A Petite Project

Skill level: Confident beginner/intermediate

Tesoritos means small treasure in Spanish. This grouping includes a tiny sewing treasures box, a pincushion, scissors sheath and fob, and rolled needlebook. The 4″ papier-mâché box is covered and lined in luscious felted wool.

SUPPLIES

These supplies are for the entire gift set.

- Black felted wool for base and backing, 13″ × 13″
- Weeks Dye Works felted wool (*or* other wool fabric in similar colors):
  Purple Rain (bright purple), 3″ × 3½″
  Pumpkin (orange), 1″ × 2″
  Lemon Chiffon (bright yellow), 1″ × 2″
  Chartreuse (bright yellow-green), 4″ × 4½″
  Candy Apple (bright red), 1″ × 2″
  Bubble Gum (bright pink), 12″ × 12″
- Medici wool thread in white
- Weeks Dye Works wool thread:
  Banana Popsicle (yellow)
  Chartreuse (bright yellow-green)
  Turquoise
  Pumpkin (orange)
  Bubble Gum (bright pink)
- Vineyard wool thread in Fern (bright green)
- Bella Lusso wool thread in Blueberry 229 (blue)
- Milliners, chenille, and embroidery needles
- Paper punch
- Orange silk ribbon, 18″
- Papier-mâché box, 4″ diameter
- Elmer's School Glue

- 1″ paintbrush
- Polyester batting
- White and black quilting thread
- Mini drill for making twisted cord
- Tart tin, 2½″ diameter
- Polyester craft stuffing
- Glue gun and glue sticks

Mini Treasure Box

Finished size: 4″ diameter

Prework

Refer to the placement guide pattern (page 29) and to Refresh Me (page 88) for detailed instructions.

1. Create a clear vinyl placement guide.

2. Create a tissue-paper embroidery guide.

3. Prepare the base fabric, adding a stitched line as a guide for the live area for appliqué and to help you accurately position the top piece when constructing the box.

Construction

Refer to Refresh Me (page 88) for detailed instructions on freezer-paper patterns and the slanted-needle technique. Refer to Stitching Glossary (page 95) for an illustration of each stitch.

STEP ONE: BEGIN THE EMBROIDERY

1. Position the embroidery guide and pin in place. Stitch the embroidery guide, using Chartreuse sewing thread.

2. Embroider the spiral stems, using 2 lengths of Chartreuse wool thread. Chainstitch the spirals over the stitches made with the embroidery guide.

Note

It's important to stitch the spiral stems before you place the wool appliqué shapes. Once the spirals are stitched, you can place the other shapes accurately.

STEP TWO: PREPARING FOR APPLIQUÉ

1. Referring to the patterns (page 29), use freezer-paper methods to create the wool appliqué shapes. Wait to create the small circles until you are ready to embroider them to the base.

2. Line up and hinge the placement guide on top of the felted wool base, securing with straight pins along the top edge.

3. Place the appliqué shapes in position and pin.

4. Baste all shapes, using white cotton thread and a milliners needle.

STEP THREE: APPLIQUÉ

1. Using blue wool thread, appliqué the flower using the slanted needle technique. Follow the stitching diagram (page 29) to make sure the flower is appliquéd straight.

2. Appliqué the Pumpkin circle to the base of the bud with Pumpkin wool thread.

STEP FOUR: FINISH THE EMBROIDERY

Leaves

Embellish the leaves with Vineyard bright green thread. Begin with the stem stitch down the center of the leaf. Use a straight stitch on the side veins as shown on the placement guide.

Beginning at the base of the center vein, needle up and then down at a slant, creating the veins on the right side on the way up, and the veins on the left side on the way down. To make these veins accurate, follow the arrows on the *Tesoros* leaves stitching illustration (page 12).

Circles and Knots

1. Using a paper punch, create small circles of color as follows:

- Lemon Chiffon for the spiral buds (Cut 2.)
- Candy Apple for the flower and bud centers (Cut 2.)

2. Punch the circles using the freezer paper method, as it will be easier for the punch to cut when the fabric is stabilized with the freezer paper. The paper punch method does not cut all the way through on at least one side, so use sharp embroidery scissors to cut the rest of the circle from the fabric. The threads will be weakened from the punch and should be easy to see.

3. Embroider a line of stem stitching in white wool thread around the flower and bud.

4. Using a double length of turquoise wool thread, stitch elongated lazy daisy stitches inside the petals on the Purple Rain flowers and buds. Add a straight stitch to fill the middle of the lazy daisy. Use a stab stitch motion to get these stitches to lie correctly.

5. Using this same thread, affix the Candy Apple circle to the center of the Pumpkin base circle on the bud, using a single colonial knot. Do the same for the 2 Lemon Chiffon circles on the spiral stems.

6. Using a double length of Bubble Gum thread, add colonial knots to the center of each petal edge and make the lazy daisy flowers on each side. Add a colonial knot in turquoise to the center of these small flowers. Using a double length of Pumpkin thread, add colonial knots to the spiral stems following the placement guide and affix the Candy Apple circle to the flower.

7. Using a single length of white wool thread, add straight stitches between the petals on the flowers and buds to delineate the petals.

STEP FIVE: FINISHING THE BOX

Refer to Making Covered Boxes (page 84) for detailed directions on finishing the box.

Rolled Needlebook

Finished size: 2½″ × 4¾″ open

Prework

Refer to the placement guide pattern (page 30) and to Refresh Me (page 88) for detailed instructions.

1. Create a clear vinyl placement guide.

2. Create a tissue-paper embroidery guide for the spiral stems.

3. Prepare the base fabric.

Construction

Refer to Refresh Me (page 88) for detailed instructions on freezer-paper patterns and the slanted-needle technique. Refer to Stitching Glossary (page 95) for an illustration of each stitch.

STEP ONE: PREPARING FOR APPLIQUÉ

1. Referring to the patterns (page 29), use freezer-paper methods to create the wool appliqué shapes.

Use a paper punch to cut 2 Lemon Chiffon circles for the spiral buds.

2. Line up and hinge the placement guide at the top of the felted wool base, securing with straight pins along the top edge.

3. Position the embroidery guide and pin in place. Remove the placement guide and stitch the embroidery guide, using Chartreuse sewing thread.

4. Reposition and hinge the placement guide at the top of the wool base.

5. Place the appliqué shapes in position and pin.

6. Baste all shapes, using white cotton thread and a milliners needle.

STEP TWO: APPLIQUÉ

Using matching wool threads, appliqué the shapes in place on the front of the needlebook. For dimension in your appliqué, use the needle-slanting technique.

STEP THREE: EMBROIDERY

Embellish the design, using the same methods as in the *Tesoritos* box top (page 23).

STEP FOUR: ASSEMBLY

1. Position, pin, and baste the Chartreuse wool lining to the inside front, and the bright pink lining piece to the inside back, lining them up with the top and sides of the book. There will be space between them for a spine, making it easier to fold.

2. Using a length of black perle cotton #8, blanket stitch the outer edges, leaving the inside edges open to be used as pockets.

3. Use the silk ribbon to secure the book, which can be rolled (to fit into the box easily) or used in book format.

Add some needles to the book and it's done—a soft and easy-to-use needlebook for you or a stitching friend.

Pincushion

Finished size: 2½″ diameter

Prework

Refer to the placement guide pattern (page 30) and to Refresh Me (page 88) for detailed instructions.

1. Create a clear vinyl placement guide.

2. Prepare the base fabric.

Construction

Refer to Refresh Me (page 88) for detailed instructions on freezer-paper patterns and the slanted-needle technique. Refer to Stitching Glossary (page 95) for an illustration of each stitch.

STEP ONE: PREPARING FOR APPLIQUÉ

1. Referring to the patterns (page 29), use freezer-paper methods to create the wool appliqué shapes.

Use a paper punch to cut a Candy Apple circle for the flower.

2. Position, pin, and baste the flower in the center.

STEPS TWO AND THREE: APPLIQUÉ AND EMBROIDERY

1. Appliqué and embellish the design, using the same methods as in the previous *Tesoritos* projects.

2. In addition, use Chartreuse wool thread to surround the flower in small lazy daisy stitches.

STEP FOUR: ASSEMBLY

1. Cut out the circle along the white line.

2. Using a milliners needle and a double length of quilting thread, stitch a running stitch along the perimeter about ¼″ from the edge.

3. Place a good-sized ball of craft stuffing inside and gather the base into a ball. Once you are pleased with the amount of stuffing, secure the quilting thread and tie off tightly by running extra stitches through again a few times and securing with a knot.

4. Using a glue gun, place a healthy amount of glue on the inside edges and bottom of the tart tin and press the appliquéd, stuffed ball inside.

Add a few pins and you're done!

Mini Scissors Sheath and Fob

Finished sheath: 2″ × 2½″ • **Finished fob:** 5″ long

Prework

Prepare the base fabrics by creating freezer-paper patterns for the outer and lining pieces of the tiny scissors sheath. The lining pieces for the front and back are slightly smaller than the exterior pieces, so be careful to use the appropriate pattern for all 4 pieces.

Construction

There is no need for an placement guide since the project is so small. Just eyeball it, but refer to the placement guide pattern (page 30). Refer to Stitching Glossary (page 95) for an illustration of each stitch.

STEP ONE: EMBROIDERY

Embellish with lazy daisy stitches in turquoise, chain stitches in Chartreuse, and colonial knots in Pumpkin and Bubble Gum wool thread.

STEP TWO: ASSEMBLY

1. Position the front, Chartreuse lining, Bubble Gum lining, and back in a sandwich and baste together, using white cotton thread.

2. Using a length of black perle cotton #8, blanket stitch the side edges, securing the corners with 3 or 4 stitches in the high stress areas.

3. At the beginning of the curve, stitch only the Chartreuse lining and black front, then the Bubble Gum lining and the black back.

THE SCISSORS FOB

1. The scissors fob is a twisted cord made from Chartreuse wool thread. The general rule for making twisted cord is to cut the threads to be used 3 times longer than the finished cord. For this cord, use 15″ for a 5″ finished cord, using 4 lengths of Chartreuse wool thread. See Making Twisted Cord (page 87).

2. Knot the end of the twisted cord and secure on the scissors handle, using a slip knot.

Tesoritos (all projects)

Do not cut.

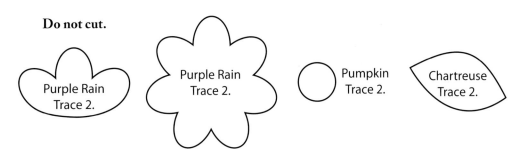

Purple Rain
Trace 2.

Purple Rain
Trace 2.

Pumpkin
Trace 2.

Chartreuse
Trace 2.

Tesoritos Mini Treasure Box

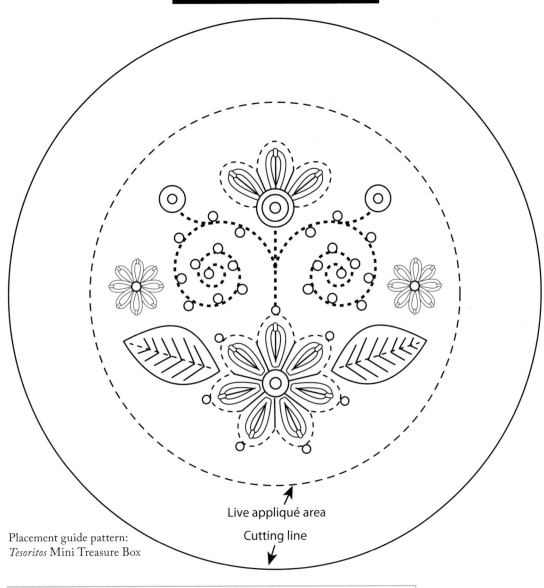

Live appliqué area

Cutting line

Placement guide pattern:
Tesoritos Mini Treasure Box

Stem Stitch - - - - - - -	Chain Stitch ••••••••••
Grouped Lazy Daisy	Lazy Daisy
Colonial Knot **O**	Straight Stitch ——————

Tesoritos **Rolled Needlebook**

Fold line

Placement guide pattern:
Tesoritos Rolled Needlebook

Stem Stitch	- - - - -
Chain Stitch	▪ ▪ ▪ ▪ ▪
Lazy Daisy	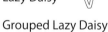
Grouped Lazy Daisy	
Colonial Knot	O
Straight Stitch	————

Tesoritos **Mini Scissors Sheath**

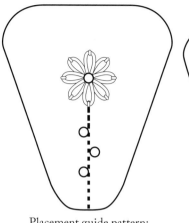

Do not cut.

Lining only
Bubble Gum
Chartreuse
Trace 1 each.

Placement guide pattern:
Tesoritos Mini Scissors Sheath

Tesoritos **Pincushion**

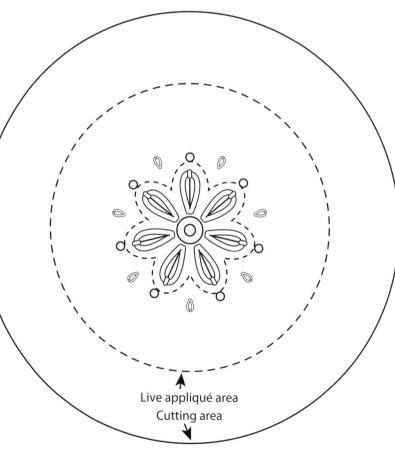

Live appliqué area
Cutting area

Placement guide pattern: *Tesoritos* Pincushion

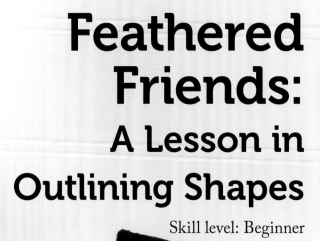

Feathered Friends:
A Lesson in Outlining Shapes

Skill level: Beginner

The proverb "Birds of a feather flock together" can be traced back to the sixteenth century. It has been used in writing to mean people of the same taste and interest will be inclined to congregate together. In fact, birds of the same species do flock together, so the proverb is rooted in truth. It is the same with those of us who like to hand sew, as we love to be with others who have the same interest.

This design features two birds that, although they have different coloring, have much in common. The symmetry, heart, and frame of leaves symbolize a growing, loving friendship.

When designing this grouping, I added outline stitching in perle cotton #8 to clarify and add dimension to the shapes.

Table Mat

Finished size: 14½″ diameter

SUPPLIES

- Black felted wool for base and backing, 17″ × 34″

- Weeks Dye Works felted wool (or other wool fabric in similar colors):
  Merlot (deep red), 9″ × 10″
  Mustard (golden yellow), 2½″ × 3″
  Collards (dark green), 5″ × 8″
  Blue Topaz (bright blue), 4″ × 5½″
  Deep Sea (dark blue), 4″ × 5½″

- Weeks Dye Works wool thread in Saffron (light gold) and Turquoise

- Bella Lusso wool threads in Pine 675 (green) and Chianti 576 (burgundy)

- Painter's Thread wool thread in Renoir (blue, overdyed)

- DMC perle cotton #8 in Gold 742, Red 321, and black

- Milliners, chenille, and embroidery needles

Prework

Refer to the placement guide pattern (pullout page P2) and to Refresh Me (page 88) for detailed instructions.

1. Create a clear vinyl placement guide.

2. Prepare the base fabric.

Construction

Refer to Refresh Me (page 88) for detailed instructions on freezer-paper patterns and the slanted-needle technique.
Refer to Stitching Glossary (page 95) for an illustration of each stitch.

STEP ONE: PREPARING FOR APPLIQUÉ

1. Referring to the patterns (pages 37 and 38), use freezer-paper methods to create the wool appliqué shapes.

2. Line up and hinge the placement guide at the top of the felted wool base, securing with 3–5 straight pins along the top edge.

3. Place the appliqué shapes in position and pin.

4. Baste all shapes, using white cotton thread and a milliners needle.

STEP TWO: APPLIQUÉ

1. Appliqué the shapes with matching threads and a chenille needle, using the slanted needle technique.

2. Begin appliquéing the birds at their beaks, making sure they are aligned.

3. When appliquéing the hearts, follow the stitch order in the stitching diagram.

Stitching diagram

STEP THREE: EMBROIDERY

Using the stem stitch and perle cotton #8, outline the hearts.

---

tips Successful Outlining

Here are a few guides for successful outlining, using the stem stitch:

- *Use enough thread to completely outline most small shapes so you will not have to start and stop.*

- *When using longer threads, trim the end when it becomes frayed to prevent the tail twisting around the working thread.*

- *Untwist your thread regularly by twirling between your thumb and index finger or by dropping the needle and allowing it to spin. This will help to avoid knots.*

STEP FOUR: ASSEMBLY

1. Place the completed appliquéd base face-up on top of a piece of wool large enough to accommodate the entire piece. Pin in place.

2. Using a milliners needle and white cotton thread, baste along the entire perimeter at least ¼˝ away from edge.

3. Trim the scalloped edge, cutting away the white line marking the base shape as you go. It will be easier to return and clip the interior valley points afterward.

4. Using black perle cotton, blanket stitch the entire perimeter.

Voila! Enjoy the table mat.

Composition Book Cover

Finished size: 7½″ × 10″ closed, 15″ × 10″ open

SUPPLIES

- Black felted wool for base, 12″ × 23″

- Weeks Dye Works felted wool (*or other wool fabric in similar colors*):
  Merlot (deep red), 5″ × 6″
  Mustard (golden yellow), 2″ × 2″
  Collards (dark green), 3″ × 5″
  Blue Topaz (bright blue), 3″ × 3″
  Deep Sea (dark blue), 3″ × 3″

- Weeks Dye Works wool threads in Saffron (light gold) and Turquoise

- Painter's Thread wool thread in Renoir (blue, overdyed)

- DMC perle cotton #8 in Gold 742, Red 321, and black

- Black satin ribbon, ½″ wide, 1 yard

- Valdani perle cotton #8 in Green Pastures 526 (green, overdyed)

- Milliners, chenille, and embroidery needles

- Mead College-Ruled Composition Book, 7½″ × 9¾″

Prework

Refer to the placement guide pattern (pullout page P2) and to Refresh Me (page 88) for detailed instructions.

1. Create a clear vinyl placement guide for just the front panel.

2. Prepare the base fabric.

The book cover pattern is for a book that measures 7½″ × 9¾″ closed and features a ¾″ spine and 3″ flaps. Measure the book you intend to cover and adjust before you begin. For a book this exact size, start with a base shape 10¼″ × 21¾″ and use the placement guide to help you position the appliqué from the right edge of the base.

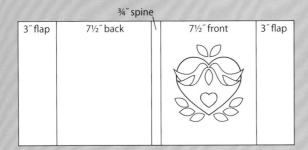

Construction

Refer to Refresh Me (page 88) for detailed instructions on freezer-paper patterns and the slanted-needle technique. Refer to Stitching Glossary (page 95) for an illustration of each stitch.

STEP ONE: PREPARING FOR APPLIQUÉ

1. Referring to the patterns (page 38), use freezer-paper methods to create the wool appliqué shapes.

2. Line up and hinge the placement guide 3″ in from the right edge of the felted wool base, securing with 3–5 straight pins along the top edge.

3. Place the appliqué shapes in position and pin.

4. Baste all shapes, using white cotton thread and a milliners needle.

STEP TWO: APPLIQUÉ

1. Using matching threads and a chenille needle, appliqué the shapes.

2. Begin appliquéing the birds at the beaks to make sure they are aligned. Begin the center leaf at the top, aligning it with the bird beaks.

3. When appliquéing the hearts, follow the stitching progression shown in the *Feathered Friends* Table Mat stitching diagram (page 33).

STEP THREE: EMBROIDERY

Using a stem stitch and perle cotton #8, outline the hearts. Stay close to the shape to increase the dimension of the shape. See the directions for stitching around the hearts in *Feathered Friends* Table Mat, Step Three: Embroidery (page 33).

STEP FOUR: FINISHING

1. Fit the cover to your composition book to be sure when you sew the flaps, the cover will remain tight. Pin.

2. Beginning on the top inside edge of the cover, blanket stitch the flap securely. Continue blanket stitching across the top, stitching the flap securely at the inside right edge as well. Repeat on the bottom, making sure to bury your knots inside the flaps.

3. Position a 17″ length of ¼″ black satin ribbon on the center of the front flap. Whipstitch both sides of the ribbon for the length of the 3″ flap. Repeat on the back flap. Tie the book closed, using the ribbon.

Large Needlebook

Finished size: 5″ × 5″

SUPPLIES

- Black felted wool for base, 11″ × 11″
- Weeks Dye Works felted wool (*or* other wool fabric in similar colors):
  Merlot (deep red): 11″ × 8″
  Mustard (golden yellow): 4½″ × 5″
  Collards (dark green): 2½″ × 2½″
  Blue Topaz (bright blue): 2½″ × 3½″
  Deep Sea (dark blue): 2½″ × 3½″
- Weeks Dye Works wool threads in Saffron (light gold) and Turquoise
- Painter's Thread wool thread in Renoir (blue, overdyed)
- DMC perle cotton #8 in Gold 742, Red 321, and black
- Milliners, chenille, and embroidery needles
- Black satin ribbon, ¼″ wide, ½ yard

Prework

Refer to the placement guide pattern (pages 39 and 40) and to Refresh Me (page 88) for detailed instructions.

1. Create clear placement guides for the cover and 1 inside panel.

2. Prepare the base fabric by cutting the black wool in the following sizes:

- 1 rectangle 4¾″ × 9½″
- 2 rectangles 4¾″ × 4⅝″

Construction

Refer to Refresh Me (page 88) for detailed instructions on freezer-paper patterns and the slanted-needle technique.
Refer to Stitching Glossary (page 95) for an illustration of each stitch.

STEP ONE: PREPARING FOR APPLIQUÉ

1. Refer to the patterns (pages 39 and 40). Use freezer-paper methods to create the wool appliqué shapes.

2. Line up and hinge the placement guide for the front cover, securing with 3 straight pins along the top edge. Place the hearts, birds, wings, and leaves into position. Pin and baste.

3. Position the placement guide for the inside panels. Place the hearts and eyeball the top leaves, pinning and basting them into place.

STEP TWO: APPLIQUÉ

1. Using matching wool threads, appliqué the shapes in place on the outside cover and both inside panels.

2. When appliquéing the hearts, use the stitch progression shown in the *Feathered Friends* Table Mat stitching diagram (page 33).

STEP THREE: EMBROIDERY

Outline the hearts with DMC perle #8, using a stem stitch and a chenille needle. See Tips: Successful Outlining (page 33).

STEP FOUR: ASSEMBLY

1. Line up the inside panels with the left and right edges of the outside piece, wrong sides together, and baste the perimeter.

2. Tuck at least ¾″ of the ends of 8½″ lengths of ¼″ black satin ribbon into both outside edges for the ties.

3. Using black DMC perle cotton #8, blanket stitch the perimeter catching the ties securely and burying your knots between the layers.

Add some needles and voila!

Alternate Ideas

Use the *Feathered Friends* pattern to cover the lid and sides of a small box. See Making Covered Boxes (page 84) for construction details. To make your gift box even more special, rearrange a few appliqué elements to make new versions of the *Tesoritos* Mini Scissors Sheath (page 28) and *Tesoritos* Needlebook (page 25) to tuck inside.

The heart becomes a whimsical flower in this version of the *Tesoros* Scissors Sheath and Fob (page 17). A single bird and heart make a really sweet option for the top of the *Tesoros* Pincushion (page 16).

And a small version of the bird and heart look perfect on this checkbook cover. To make the cover, see the construction details in the *Feathered Friends* Composition

Book Cover (page 34) and adjust the measurements to fit your checks and register. Measuring a generic plastic register may help you come up with the correct measurements.

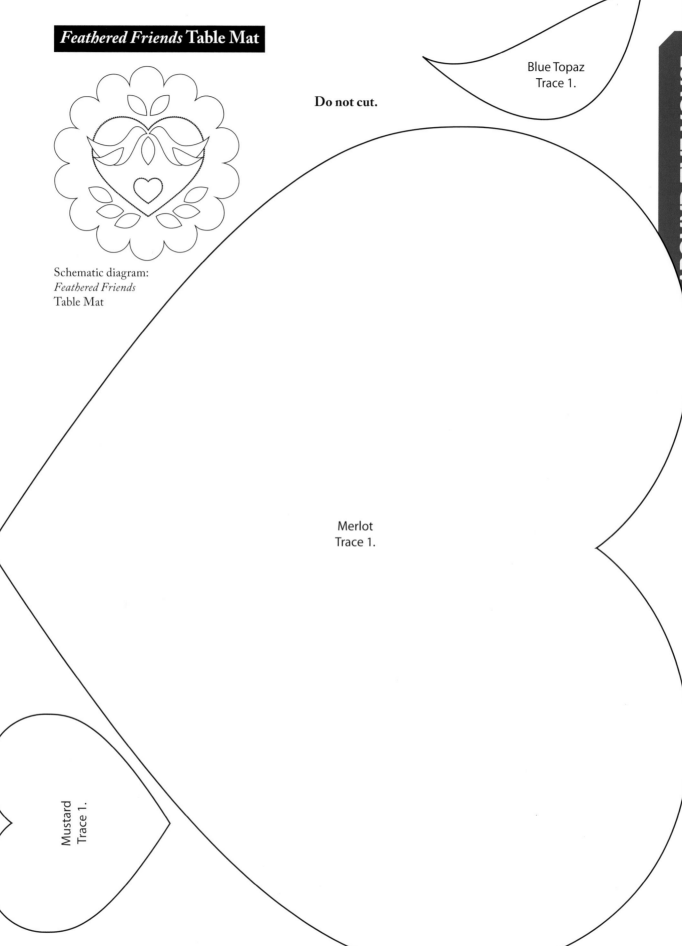

Feathered Friends **Table Mat**

Schematic diagram:
Feathered Friends
Table Mat

Do not cut.

Blue Topaz
Trace 1.

Merlot
Trace 1.

Mustard
Trace 1.

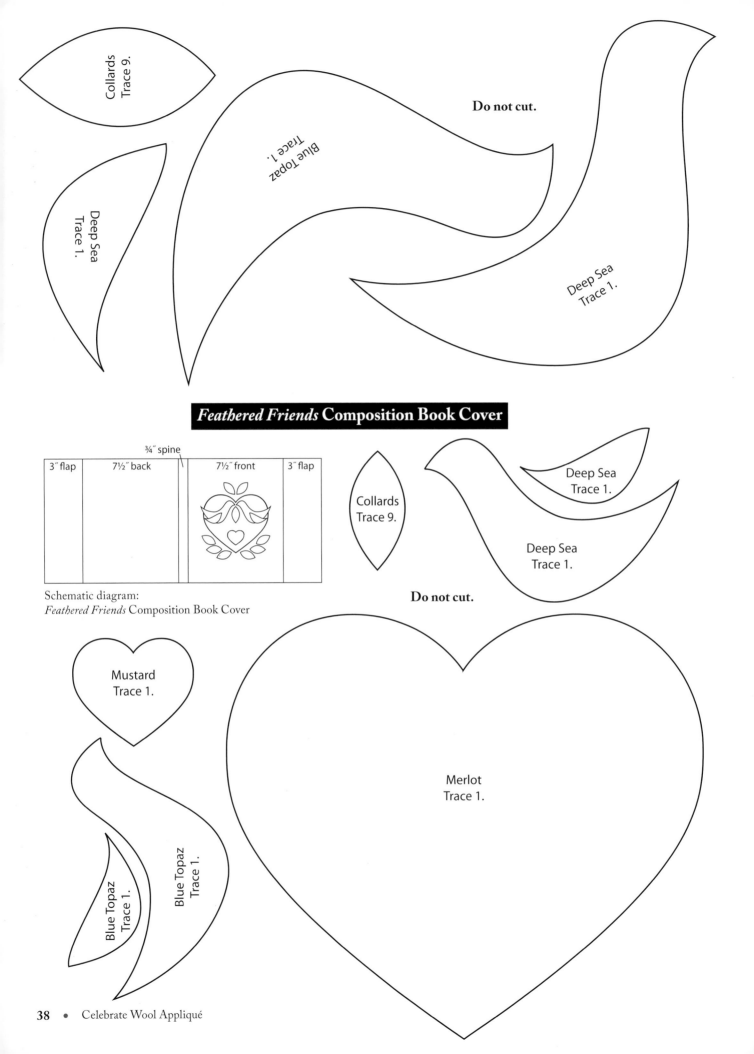

Collards
Trace 9.

Deep Sea
Trace 1.

Blue Topaz
Trace 1.

Do not cut.

Deep Sea
Trace 1.

Feathered Friends Composition Book Cover

3″ flap	7½″ back	7½″ front	3″ flap

¾″ spine

Schematic diagram:
Feathered Friends Composition Book Cover

Collards
Trace 9.

Deep Sea
Trace 1.

Deep Sea
Trace 1.

Do not cut.

Mustard
Trace 1.

Merlot
Trace 1.

Blue Topaz
Trace 1.

Blue Topaz
Trace 1.

Feathered Friends Large Needlebook

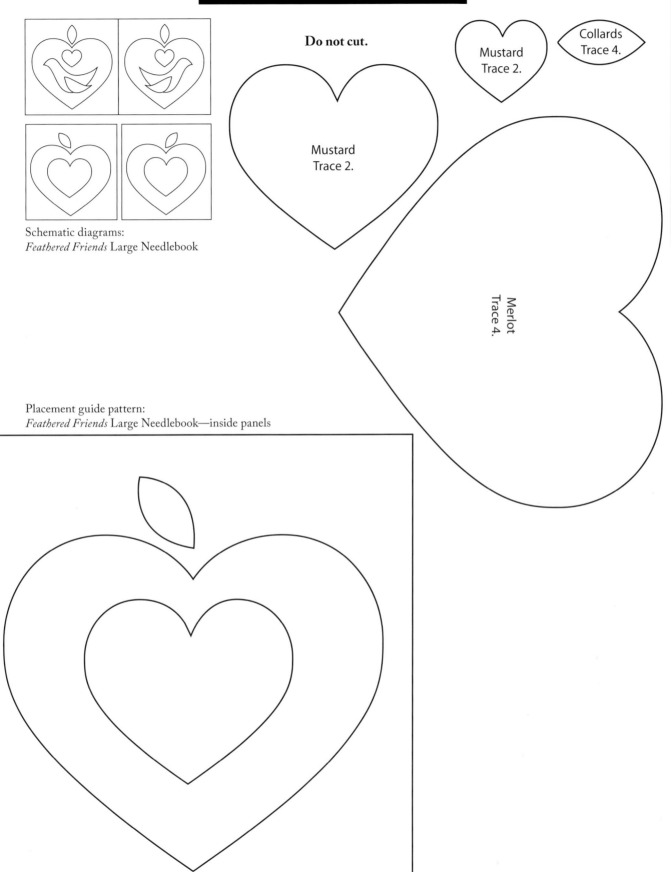

Schematic diagrams:
Feathered Friends Large Needlebook

Do not cut.

Mustard
Trace 2.

Mustard
Trace 2.

Collards
Trace 4.

Merlot
Trace 4.

Placement guide pattern:
Feathered Friends Large Needlebook—inside panels

Placement guide pattern:
Feathered Friends
Large Needlebook—
front and back cover

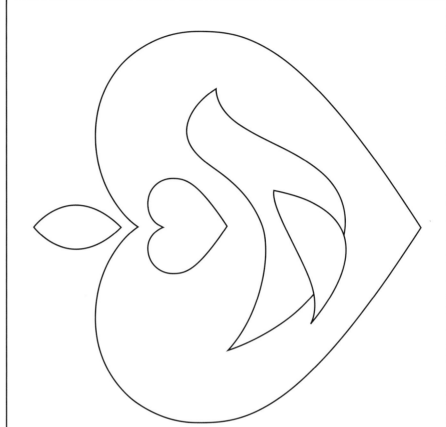

Do not cut.

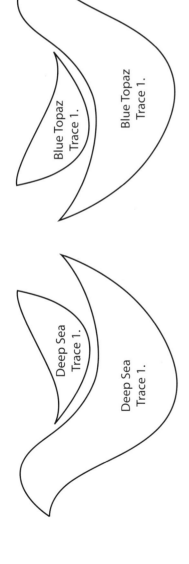

Blue Topaz
Trace 1.

Blue Topaz
Trace 1.

Deep Sea
Trace 1.

Deep Sea
Trace 1.

Holiday Laurel:
Adding Bling

Skill level: Confident beginner/intermediate

Holiday Laurel is based on a famous Baltimore Album block known as Crossed Laurel that has been given a modern holiday look. Beads, embroidery, and dimension appoint this design with sparkle and shine, making it a classic holiday decoration. The pillow, candle mat, and Christmas tree ornaments make a sweet holiday medley for seasonal decorating.

Pillow

Finished size: 15″ × 15″

SUPPLIES

- White felted wool for base, 17″ × 17″
- Weeks Dye Works Wool (*or* other wool fabric in similar colors):
  Collards (dark green), 10″ × 14″
  Merlot (deep red), 20″ × 20″
- DMC perle cotton #8 in Green 890
- Bella Lusso wool thread in Chianti 576 (burgundy) and Pine 675 (green)
- Japanese emerald lined seed beads
- 11/0 red seed beads
- C-Lon beading thread in red and green
- Milliners, chenille, embroidery, and beading needles
- Pillow form, 15″ × 15″

Construction

Refer to Refresh Me (page 88) for detailed instructions on freezer-paper patterns and the slanted-needle technique. Refer to Stitching Glossary (page 95) for an illustration of each stitch.

STEP ONE: PREPARING FOR APPLIQUÉ

1. Referring to the patterns (page 48), use freezer-paper methods to create the wool appliqué shapes.

Note: Number each shape according to the patterns. The leaves may look similar, but each is slightly different.

Prework

Refer to the placement guide pattern (pullout page P2) and to Refresh Me (page 88) for detailed instructions.

1. Create a clear vinyl placement guide.

2. Prepare the base fabric.

2. Using rotary tools, cut 2 bias strips ⁵⁄₁₆″ × 13½″ from the Collards wool fabric.

3. Line up and hinge the placement guide at the top of the felted wool base, securing with 3–5 straight pins along the top edge.

4. Position and pin the bias strips according to the placement guide. To make sure the strips are straight, pin by taking a bit out of each side of the base piece without piercing the bias strip itself.

5. Position and pin each leaf according to the placement guide and numbers for each.

6. Baste all shapes, using white cotton thread and a milliners needle.

STEPS TWO AND THREE: APPLIQUÉ

1. Appliqué the outer 3 leaves with chenille needle and burgundy wool thread, using the slanted needle technique. Begin at the base of the leaf on the right and appliqué all the way around. Then appliqué the leaf on the left to make sure they line up. Add the middle leaf.

2. Using Bella Lusso green wool thread, appliqué the bias stems, being careful to keep them straight. Using the slanted-needle stitch is not important on bias stems.

3. Using Bella Lusso green wool thread, appliqué the balance of the leaves starting at the base of each leaf and making certain the opposite leaf is lined up exactly.

STEP FOUR: EMBROIDERY

1. Using a chenille needle and DMC green perle cotton, chainstitch down the middle of each bias stem working the top stem first.

2. Chainstitch the second stem, slipping the needle under the crossed area and picking up the stitch on the other side.

STEP FIVE: ADDING BEADS

1. Using a length of red C-Lon thread and a beading needle, add 6 beads evenly down the center of the red leaves, being careful to attach them as straight as possible. Pull each bead tight, creating a slight dimple in the leaf. After beading each leaf, secure a knot at the end, clip and begin again on the next leaf.

2. Using green C-Lon thread, repeat for the green leaves.

3. Add emerald beads to every other chain stitch on the bias stems, being careful to nest them into the stitches.

STEP SIX: FINISHING

There are many ways to finish a pillow. The sample was finished, using covered cord in Merlot wool and the Merlot wool back features an invisible zipper, so the pillow form can be replaced. Pillows can also be sewn and turned. Use an envelope closure and then the pillow can be stuffed with craft stuffing.

Candle Mat

Finished size: 11″ × 11″

SUPPLIES

- White felted wool for base, 11″ × 11″

- Weeks Dye Works Wool (*or* other wool fabric in similar colors):

  Collards (dark green): 5″ × 8″

  Merlot (deep red): 12″ × 15″

- Bella Lusso wool thread in Chianti 576 (burgundy) and Pine 675 (green)

- Valdani perle cotton #12 in Golden Autumn 533 (red, overdyed)

- Japanese emerald lined seed beads

- 11/0 red seed beads

- C-Lon beading thread in red and green

- Milliners, chenille, embroidery, and beading needles

Prework

Refer to the placement guide pattern (pullout page P1) and to Refresh Me (page 88) for detailed instructions.

1. Create a clear vinyl placement guide.

2. Create a tissue-paper embroidery guide.

3. Prepare the base fabric.

Construction

Refer to Refresh Me (page 88) for detailed instructions on freezer-paper patterns and the slanted-needle technique. Refer to Stitching Glossary (page 95) for an illustration of each stitch.

STEP ONE: PREPARING FOR APPLIQUÉ

1. Referring to the patterns (page 48), use freezer-paper methods to create the wool appliqué shapes.

Note: Number each shape according to the patterns. The leaves may look similar, but each is slightly different.

2. Line up and hinge the placement guide at the top of the felted wool base, securing with 3–5 straight pins along the top edge.

3. Position and pin each leaf according to the placement guide and numbers for each.

4. Baste the leaves, using white cotton thread and a milliners needle.

STEP TWO: APPLIQUÉ

1. Appliqué the outer 3 leaves with a chenille needle and burgundy wool thread, using the slanted needle technique. Begin at the base of the leaf on the right and appliqué all the way around. Then appliqué the leaf on the left to make sure they line up. Add the middle leaf.

2. Using a double length of green wool thread, chainstitch the stems over the stitches made with the embroidery guide, being careful to keep them straight.

3. Using the green wool thread, appliqué the balance of the leaves starting at the base of each leaf, making certain the opposite leaf is lined up exactly.

STEP THREE: ADDING BEADS

1. Using a length of red C-Lon thread and a beading needle add 5 beads evenly down the center of the red leaves, being careful to attach them as straight as possible. Pull each bead tight, creating a slight dimple in the leaf. After beading each leaf, secure a knot at the end, clip and begin again on the next leaf.

2. Using green C-Lon thread, repeat for the green leaves.

STEP FOUR: FINISHING

Cut the finished base following the placement guide (pullout page P1). Cut the merlot backing 12″ × 12″. Blanket stitch the base to the backing, using the Valdani perle cotton. Trim the backing to make a ½″ border. Refer to Finishing a Candle Mat (page 87) for detailed instructions

Alternate Ideas

The *Holiday Laurel* pattern looks beautiful on the lid of a 15″ square box. See Making Covered Boxes (page 84) for construction details.

alternate red and green leaves for a slightly holiday look that can stay out all year in a simple pincushion.

Use a few leaves from the *Holiday Laurel* pattern to make gifts for your sewing friends. The new arrangement of red and green leaf shapes form a classic design on the *Tesoros* Needlebook (page 14) and *Tesoros* Scissors Sheath (page 17). Or, you can

Holiday Ornaments

Finished poinsettia and snowflake ornaments: 4″ diameter
Finished star ornament: 4″ × 4″ • **Finished tree ornament:** 3½″ × 5″

SUPPLIES

- White felted wool for base and backing, 10″ × 20″

- Brown felted wool, 1″ × 1″

- Weeks Dye Works wool (*or other wool fabric in similar colors*):
  Merlot (deep red), 3″ × 6″
  Collards (dark green), 4″ × 5″
  Mustard (golden yellow), 5″ × 5″

- Weeks Dye Works wool thread in Saffron (light gold)

- Wool thread or floss in brown

- Kreinik very fine #4 braid metallic thread in Red 003V and Gold 002

- DMC metallic thread in Gold E3821

- Bella Lusso wool thread in Chianti 576 (burgundy) and Pine 675 (green)

- Rainbow Gallery (RG) Silk Lamé braid SP02

- 11/0 gold beads

- 11/0 red beads

- 4mm beads in various colors for ornaments on appliqué tree

- C-Lon thread in red, green, and gold for beading

- 6/11 Czech glass beads in red, green, and gold for outer trim

- Milliners, chenille, embroidery, and beading needles

Prework

Refer to the placement guide patterns (pages 49 and 50) and to Refresh Me (page 88) for detailed instructions.

1. Create a clear vinyl placement guide for each ornament.

2. Create a tissue-paper embroidery guide for each ornament.

3. Prepare the 4 base shapes on the white wool.

Construction

Refer to Refresh Me (page 88) for detailed instructions on freezer-paper patterns and the slanted-needle technique. Refer to Stitching Glossary (page 95) for an illustration of each stitch.

STEP ONE: PREPARING FOR APPLIQUÉ

1. Referring to the patterns (pages 49 and 50), use freezer-paper methods to create the wool appliqué shapes.

2. Line up and hinge the placement guide at the top of each felted wool base, securing with straight pins along the top edge.

3. Place the appliqué shapes in position and pin.

4. Baste all shapes, using white cotton thread and a milliners needle.

STEP TWO: APPLIQUÉ

1. Using a chenille needle and burgundy wool thread, appliqué the poinsettia, red star, and Christmas tree pot, using the slanted needle technique. Leave the top of the pot open for additional dimension.

2. Using Bella Lusso green wool thread, appliqué the Christmas tree and green star.

3. Using Saffron wool thread, appliqué the star.

4. Using brown thread or floss, appliqué the tree trunk.

STEP THREE: EMBROIDERY

1. Reposition and hinge the placement guide and position the embroidery guide into place.

2. Stitch the embroidery guides as follows:

• Yellow thread for the mustard star

• Red thread for the snowflake shape

• Light gold/yellow for the Christmas tree garland

3. Using the Kreinik gold braid, stem stitch the tree garland and star lines. Using a double length, affix the tree's top star with a single colonial knot.

4. Using the Kreinik red braid, stem stitch the snowflake.

STEP FOUR: ADDING BEADS

1. Using a length of red C-Lon thread and a beading needle, add red beads evenly down the center of the poinsettia leaves, being careful to attach them as straight as possible. Pull each bead tight creating a slight dimple in the shape. After beading each leaf, secure a knot at the end before traveling to the next leaf. Add red beads to the tips of the snowflake star and one to the center.

2. Using a length of gold C-Lon thread, add gold beads to the mustard star and a cluster to the center of the poinsettia.

3. Using gold C-Lon thread, add the various colors of 4mm beads to the tree for ornaments.

STEP FIVE: FINISHING

1. To make hangers for the ornaments, follow the directions in Making Twisted Cord (page 87) to create 4 pieces of twisted cord in 8″ lengths, using DMC Gold E3821 metallic thread.

2. Place each stitched shape onto a piece of white wool. Pin and baste.

3. Cut out the 2 layers together, trimming away the base shape line.

4. Slip the raw ends of the folded, twisted cord hanger between the top edges.

5. Using a length of RG silk lamé braid in white SP02, a chenille needle, and Czech glass beads, make the outer trim. Use gold beads on the star, green on the Christmas tree, and red on the poinsettia and the snowflake.

a. Thread 1 bead.

b. Blanket stitch.

c. Pull working thread to the right, bringing the bead to the edge.

d. Repeat.

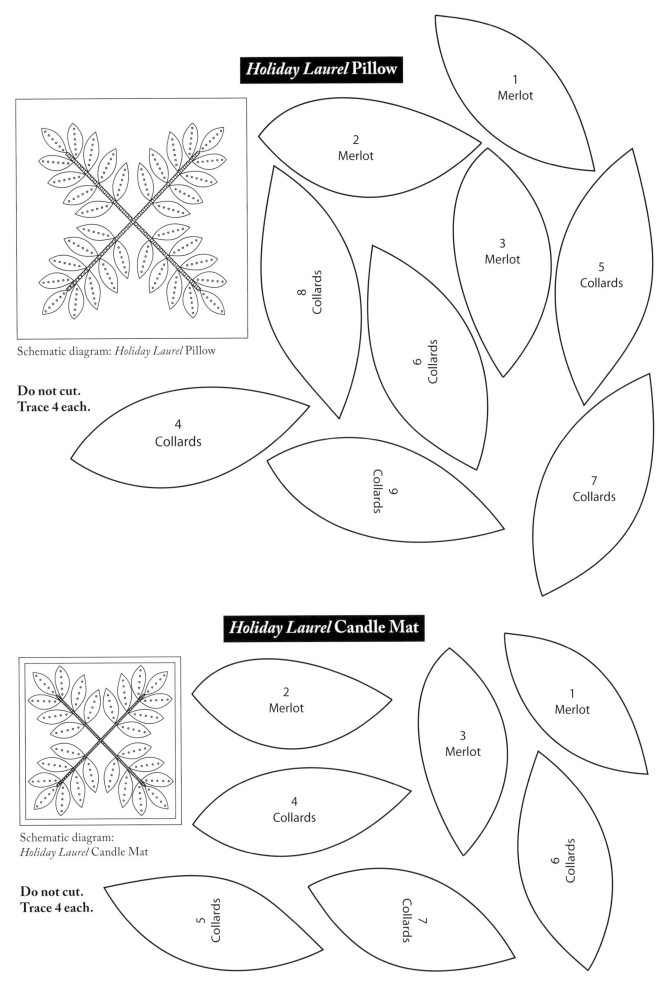

Holiday Laurel Pillow

Schematic diagram: *Holiday Laurel* Pillow

Do not cut.
Trace 4 each.

1
Merlot

2
Merlot

3
Merlot

5
Collards

8
Collards

6
Collards

4
Collards

9
Collards

7
Collards

Holiday Laurel Candle Mat

Schematic diagram:
Holiday Laurel Candle Mat

Do not cut.
Trace 4 each.

2
Merlot

1
Merlot

3
Merlot

4
Collards

6
Collards

5
Collards

7
Collards

Holiday Laurel Holiday Ornaments

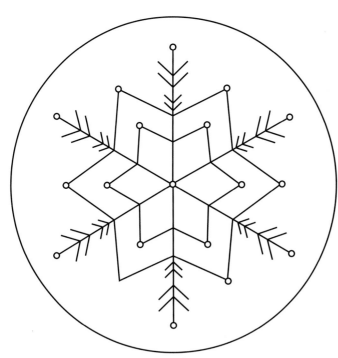

Placement guide pattern:
Holiday Laurel Holiday Ornament—snowflake

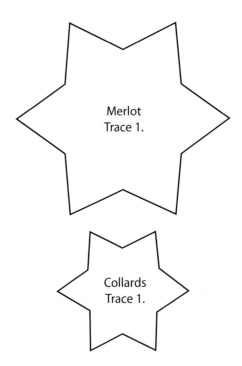

Merlot
Trace 1.

Collards
Trace 1.

Do not cut.

Placement guide pattern:
Holiday Laurel Holiday Ornament—star

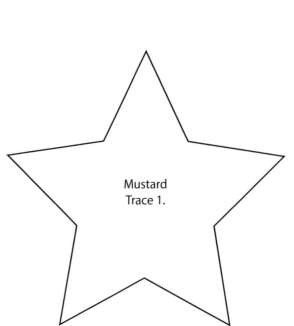

Mustard
Trace 1.

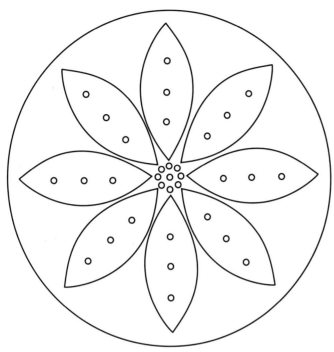

Merlot
Trace 8.

Do not cut.

Placement guide pattern:
Holiday Laurel Holiday Ornament—poinsettia

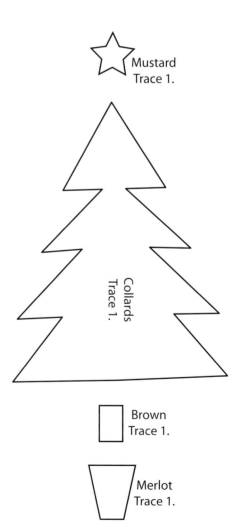

Mustard
Trace 1.

Collards
Trace 1.

Brown
Trace 1.

Merlot
Trace 1.

Placement guide pattern:
Holiday Laurel Holiday Ornament—tree

Love Birds:
A Lesson in Layering

Skill level: Beginner

These designs are based on the Pennsylvania Dutch hex sign for love and marriage. When the German, Swedish and Dutch immigrated to Pennsylvania in the seventeenth century, they brought with them a rich culture of folk art called *Fraktur*. These designs often included tulips, hearts, and distelfinks, which are stylized gold finches. Fraktur art evolved onto today's hex signs, which can be found on barns, sheds, and homes across the Pennsylvania Dutch countryside.

Wedding Banner

Finished size: 13″ × 18½″

This design features two distelfinks sitting atop an open book (perhaps a Bible) framed by laurel leaves and crowned with a heart. I chose to interpret this hex sign as a wedding or anniversary banner and made this for my niece. When she was married, the banner hung in church on the lectern to bring personalization to the marriage ceremony. It now decorates her bedroom lest the date ever be forgotten!

Instructions include finishing with hanging tabs and homespun backing.

SUPPLIES

- White felted wool for base, 15″ × 20″
- Weeks Dye Works felted wool (*or other wool fabric in similar colors*):
  Deep Sea (dark blue): 9″ × 9″
  Blue Topaz (bright blue): 4″ × 5″
  Mustard (golden yellow): 5″ × 6″
  Candy Apple (bright red): 3½″ × 4″
  Collards (dark green): 6″ × 6″

- Sewing thread to match Collards (dark green) and Deep Sea (dark blue)
- Painter's Thread wool thread in Renoir (blue, overdyed)
- Bella Lusso wool thread in Pine 675 (green)
- Weeks Dye Works wool threads in Saffron (light gold) Candy Apple (bright red), and Turquoise

- Homespun or cotton fabric, 1 fat quarter
- Pellon lightweight fusible interfacing, ½ yard
- DMC perle cotton #8 in white
- Milliners, chenille, and embroidery needles
- Rotary cutting tools

Prework

Refer to the placement guide pattern (pullout page P2) and to Refresh Me (page 88) for detailed instructions.

1. Create a clear vinyl placement guide.

2. Create a tissue-paper embroidery guide.

3. Prepare the base fabric. Save your pattern to use later for the backing.

Construction

Refer to Refresh Me (page 88) for detailed instructions on freezer-paper patterns and the slanted-needle technique. Refer to Stitching Glossary (page 95) for an illustration of each stitch.

STEP ONE: PREPARING FOR APPLIQUÉ

1. Referring to the patterns (pages 59 and 60), use freezer-paper methods to create the wool appliqué shapes.

2. Line up and hinge the placement guide at the top of the felted wool base, securing with 5 straight pins along the top edge.

3. Position the embroidery guide and pin in place. Remove the placement guide and stitch the embroidery guide, using green sewing thread accordingly.

4. Reposition and hinge the placement guide at the top of the wool base.

5. Place the appliqué shapes in position and pin. Be careful when layering the distelfink bodies and wings to be sure they are in the correct overlapping order.

6. Baste all shapes, using white cotton thread and a milliners needle.

A few hints to keep your basting effortless:

- Don't knot the thread; double the first basting stitch instead.

- Baste in straight stitches, which ultimately will make your basting stitches slant. This makes it easy to get embroidery scissors underneath and snip, easily pulling away the basting threads.

- Take care to accurately line up laurel leaves across from each other.

STEP TWO: EMBROIDERY

1. Using Renoir Painter's Thread wool thread and a chenille needle, stem stitch the lettering with a double length of thread for the names and a single length for the dates. While stitching rounded edges, make your stitches smaller for less webbing.

2. Using a double length of Collards thread, chainstitch the stems.

STEP THREE: APPLIQUÉ

Appliqué, using matching threads and the slanted needle technique to create dimension in your appliqué. This piece looks wonderful when the distelfinks are dimensional.

Here are some tips for success in appliquéing this design:

- When stitching the layered hearts, begin with the bottom heart. Sew the first 3 stitches in the top center angle, the right side of the bottom tip, and the left side of the bottom tip. Then fill in the stitches on both sides. This will help the heart stay straight. Follow the same for the next 2 hearts, making sure the tops and bottoms are lined up.

- Stitch the bottom serrated edge of the wings by stitching in between the points, leaving it a bit ragged.

- When stitching the open book, begin with the 2 center points making sure they are aligned.

- Use gold thread or floss to appliqué the beaks.

- Embroider elongated lazy daisy stitches for the crop, using turquoise wool thread. For accuracy, mark these, using the placement guide.

STEP FOUR: FINISHING

Trim the Appliqué

Using rotary cutting tools, cut the top just inside the black line. Cut the balance of the shape, eliminating the line as you trim.

Make the Lining

1. Iron the fusible interfacing to the fat quarter of homespun or cotton fabric to stabilize.

2. Using the freezer paper pattern for the base shape, trace the pattern onto the stabilized side of the backing. After peeling the freezer paper away, trim the backing adding a ⅜″ seam allowance all the way around. Fold the seam allowance along all edges and press. Use a mitered edge for the top corners.

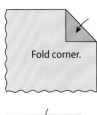

Fold corner.

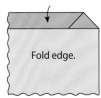

Fold edge.

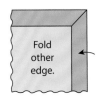

Fold other edge.

Make Tab Hangers

Using rotary cutting tools, cut a piece of the stabilized fabric 3″ × 15″. Trim the length into 3 rectangles 3″ × 5″. Press the edges in ⅜″ on the longer sides creating 3 tab hangers which can be folded and slipped in between the appliqué and the backing.

Assembly

1. Line up the completed appliqué front and the prepared backing.

2. Place the 3 tab hangers between the layers, evenly spaced across the top edge and pin. You can make the tabs shorter, depending on the hanger and/or size of dowel you will use to display the banner.

3. Pin the backing in place, making sure it does not show from the front. Baste.

4. Using white sewing thread, stab stitch tiny stitches ¼″ from the top, catching the appliqué top, tabs, and backing.

5. Using white perle cotton #8, blanket stitch the sides and bottom, catching both layers.

6. At the top of the banner, blanket stitch only the appliqué layer. This blanket stitching is only for show. The top edge is not blanket stitched for assembly as the stitches would become uneven when catching the tab hangers.

Mug Rug

Finished size: 5″ × 5″

This miniature lamb's tongue rug features the herringbone stitch. The rug is constructed to make it flat enough to balance a mug or cup securely.

SUPPLIES

- Weeks Dye Works felted wool (*or other wool fabric in similar colors*):
  Deep Sea (dark blue): 3½″ × 5″
  Mustard (golden yellow): 2½″ × 3½″
  Merlot (deep red): 3½″ × 4″
  Collards (dark green): 6″ × 10″

- Painter's Thread wool thread in Renoir (blue, overdyed)

- Bella Lusso wool thread in Pine 675 (green)

- Weeks Dye Works wool thread in Saffron (light gold)

- Milliners, chenille, and embroidery needles

- ⅝″ button to match the Merlot felted wool

Prework

Refer to the placement guide pattern (page 61) and to Refresh Me (page 88) for detailed instructions.

Make a clear vinyl placement guide.

Construction

Refer to Refresh Me (page 88) for detailed instructions on freezer-paper patterns and the slanted-needle technique. Refer to Stitching Glossary (page 95) for an illustration of each stitch.

STEP ONE: MAKING THE TONGUES

The tongue bottoms slip between the appliqué front and back, overlapping them by ¼″. All the top tongues are the same size, but the bottom pieces feature middle pieces and mitered corner pieces. Line up the tongue bottoms and tops, baste, and blanket stitch them on 3 sides. Make sure you have the corner miters matched.

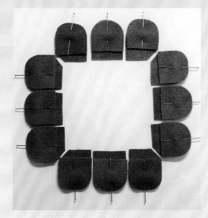

STEP TWO: PREPARING FOR APPLIQUÉ

1. Referring to the patterns (page 61), use freezer-paper methods to create the wool appliqué shapes.

2. Using rotary tools, cut a 3″ × 3″ square from both Collards and Deep Sea felted wool.

3. Line up and hinge the placement guide on top of the felted wool base, securing with 3 straight pins along the top edge.

4. Place the bottom hearts in position and pin. Position the remaining appliqué pieces and pin.

5. Baste all shapes, using white cotton thread and a milliners needle.

STEP THREE: APPLIQUÉ

1. Using matching threads and the slanted needle technique, begin appliqué with the bottom hearts. To make sure they are accurately pointed into the corners, make the first 3 stitches at the center angle, the right side of the point, and the left side of the point. Refer to the stitching diagram in the *Love Birds Wedding Banner* (page 54).

2. Appliqué the top hearts, using the same method.

3. Secure the center circle with the button and a double length of Saffron thread for a splash of color.

STEP FOUR: ASSEMBLY

1. Using a milliners needle and white basting thread, baste the tongues in position.

2. Flip the work over and baste the bottom square over the tongues on the back. Using matching thread and a running stitch, secure the back in place catching the tongues.

3. Flip back to the front and use matching wool thread and a chenille needle to stitch the entire perimeter, using a herringbone stitch. Make sure to catch the tongues in the stitching.

Alternate Color Ideas

Coffee Cuff

Finished size: 5″ × 11″

Keep your hands and your coffee warm with this lush coffee collar. The design features a Velcro closure, blanket-stitch construction, and will fit most twelve-ounce hot cups.

SUPPLIES

- Black or white felted wool for base and backing, 10″ × 12″
- Weeks Dye Works felted wool (or other wool fabric in similar colors):

  Collards (dark green): 2½″ × 7″

  Candy Apple (bright red): 3″ × 3½″

  Mustard (golden yellow): 2½″ × 2½″

  Deep Sea (dark blue): 2″ × 2″
- Weeks Dye Works wool threads in Saffron (light gold) and Candy Apple (bright red)
- Bella Lusso wool thread in Pine 675 (green)
- Painter's Thread wool thread in Renoir (blue overdyed)
- Perle cotton #8 in black or white to match wool background
- Milliners, chenille, and embroidery needles
- Hook-and-loop tape, ½″ strip in black or white to match wool background

Prework

Refer to the placement guide pattern (page 62) and to Refresh Me (page 88) for detailed instructions.

1. Create a clear vinyl placement guide.

2. Create a tissue-paper embroidery guide.

3. Prepare the base fabric.

Construction

Refer to Refresh Me (page 88) for detailed instructions on freezer-paper patterns and the slanted-needle technique. Refer to Stitching Glossary (page 95) for an illustration of each stitch.

STEP ONE: PREPARING FOR APPLIQUÉ

1. Referring to the patterns (page 61), use freezer-paper methods to create the appliqué shapes.

2. Line up and hinge the placement guide on the felted wool base, securing with straight pins along the top edge.

3. Position, pin, and baste all shapes, using white cotton thread and a milliners needle.

STEP TWO: EMBROIDERY

Using a double length of green wool thread, chainstitch the stems over the stitches made with the embroidery guide.

STEP THREE: APPLIQUÉ

Using matching threads and a chenille needle, appliqué the shapes, using the slanted needle technique. For increased accuracy, follow these guidelines.

• Begin stitching the leaves at the base near the stem to align them accurately.

• Follow the stitching diagram for the heart in the *Love Birds* Wedding Banner (page 54).

STEP FOUR: ASSEMBLY

1. Place the piece of black or white felted wool fabric behind the completed appliqué and pin the perimeter. Using white cotton thread and a milliner's needle, baste the perimeter of the cuff at least ¼″ inside the base shape line.

2. Cut out both layers together, trimming away the base shape line.

3. Using perle cotton #8 in black or white, blanket stitch the perimeter of the cuff.

4. Add 2″ lengths of hook-and-loop tape to the overlapping ends for a snug fit. Once they are positioned, stitch to secure the hook-and-loop tape.

Alternate Ideas

Use the *Love Birds* appliqué pattern to make a beautiful large round box. See Making Covered Boxes (page 84) for construction details.

Love Birds Wedding Banner

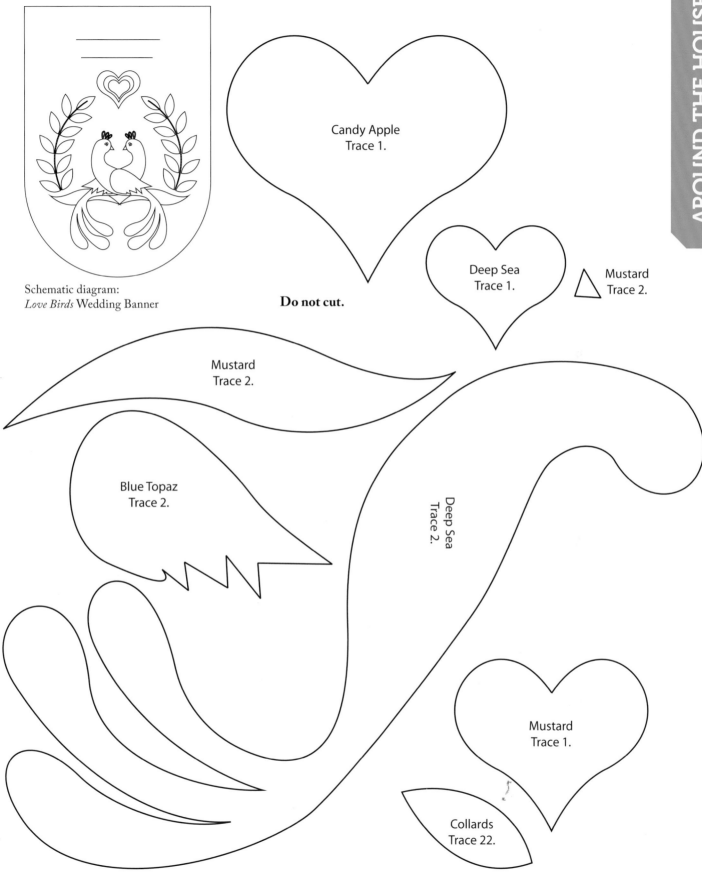

Schematic diagram:
Love Birds Wedding Banner

**Candy Apple
Trace 1.**

Do not cut.

**Deep Sea
Trace 1.**

**Mustard
Trace 2.**

**Mustard
Trace 2.**

**Blue Topaz
Trace 2.**

**Deep Sea
Trace 2.**

**Mustard
Trace 1.**

**Collards
Trace 22.**

59

ABCDEFGHI
JKLMNOPQR
STUVWXYZ

ABCDEFGHIJKN
OPQRSTUVWXYZ
123456789028

abcdefghijklm
nopqrstuvwxyz

abcdefghijklmnop
qrstuvwxyz

Love Birds Mug Rug

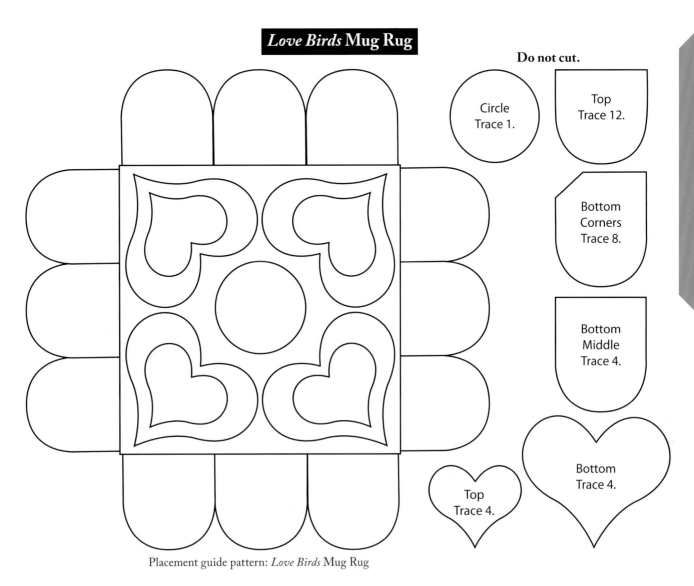

Do not cut.

Circle
Trace 1.

Top
Trace 12.

Bottom
Corners
Trace 8.

Bottom
Middle
Trace 4.

Top
Trace 4.

Bottom
Trace 4.

Placement guide pattern: *Love Birds* Mug Rug

Love Birds Coffee Cuff

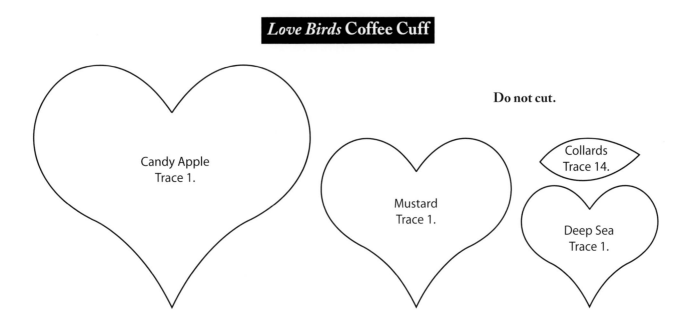

Do not cut.

Candy Apple
Trace 1.

Mustard
Trace 1.

Collards
Trace 14.

Deep Sea
Trace 1.

Placement guide pattern: *Love Birds* Coffee Cuff

| Chain Stitch | ----------- |

Wine Country:
Working with Embroidery Guides

Skill level: Beginner

This suite of wool accessories for wine is a wonderful accent to any wine and cheese party. The collection includes a wine bottle mat and bottle snug, coasters, wine glass charms and a decorative, unlined box to house them when not in use. These items are both easy and fun and make wonderful gifts for yourself or a friend.

Storage Box

Finished size: 8″ diameter

SUPPLIES

- Black felted wool for base, 18″ × 27″

- Weeks Dye Works felted wool (*or other wool fabric in similar colors*):
  Collards (dark green), 6″ × 9″
  Bordeaux (dark magenta), 5″ × 5″

- Weeks Dye Works wool thread in Ivy (green, overdyed)

- Caron Impressions wool/silk thread in Cherry (overdyed)

- 10/0 transparent Delica beads in Lilac

- C-Lon thread in Lilac for beading

- DMC perle cotton #8 in black

- Milliners, chenille, embroidery, and beading needles

- Papier-mâché box, 8″ diameter

- Elmer's School Glue

- 1″ paintbrush

- Polyester batting

- White and black quilting thread

Prework

Refer to the placement guide pattern (pullout page P1) and to Refresh Me (page 88) for detailed instructions.

1. Create a clear vinyl placement guide.

2. Create a tissue-paper embroidery guide.

3. Prepare the base fabric, adding a stitched line as a guide for the live area for appliqué and to help you accurately position the top piece when constructing the box.

Make the Box Lid

Refer to Refresh Me (page 88) for detailed instructions on freezer-paper patterns and the slanted-needle technique. Refer to Stitching Glossary (page 95) for an illustration of each stitch.

STEP ONE: PREPARING FOR APPLIQUÉ

1. Referring to the patterns (page 70), use freezer-paper methods to create the wool appliqué shapes.

2. Line up and hinge the placement guide at the top of the felted wool base, securing with 3–5 straight pins along the top edge.

3. Position the embroidery guide and pin in place. Remove the placement guide and stitch the embroidery guide, using green thread.

4. Reposition and hinge the placement guide at the top of the fabric base.

5. Place the appliqué shapes in position and pin.

6. Baste all shapes, using white cotton thread and a milliners needle.

STEP TWO: APPLIQUÉ

1. Using a chenille needle and Cherry thread, appliqué the grapes, using the slanted-needle technique.

2. Using a chenille needle and Ivy thread, appliqué the leaves, using the slanted-needle technique.

STEP THREE: EMBROIDERY AND BEADS

1. Continuing with Ivy thread, embroider the vines using a chain stitch and the small curls using a stem stitch.

2. Mark the leaves with vein lines, using a running stitch, or use a Micron pen to make a dotted line.

3. Embroider the veins on the leaves in Ivy thread.

4. Using lilac C-Lon thread and a beading needle, add the transparent lilac beads to the grapes as shown on the placement guide.

Make the Box Side

STEP ONE: PREPARING FOR APPLIQUÉ

Referring to the directions for the box top:

1. Position and stitch the embroidery guide.

2. Create the appliqué shapes for the leaves.

3. Hinge the placement guide. Position, pin, and baste the leaves in place.

STEP TWO: APPLIQUÉ AND EMBROIDERY

1. Appliqué the leaves, using the Ivy thread.

2. Continuing with the Ivy thread, embroider the vines using the chain stitch and the curls using the stem stitch.

Finishing

Refer to Making Covered Boxes (page 84) for detailed directions on finishing the box.

Serving Mat and Coasters

Finished mat: 6¼″ diameter • **Finished coaster:** 4″ diameter

These five items can be worked on the same piece of wool and cut apart later when backing. Or use scraps of black wool and make each as a separate piece.

SUPPLIES

- Black felted wool for base and backing, 15″ × 20″
- Weeks Dye Works felted wool (*or other wool fabric in similar colors*): Collards (dark green), 6″ × 9″ Bordeaux (dark magenta), 5″ × 5″
- Weeks Dye Works wool thread in Ivy (green, overdyed)
- Caron Impressions silk/wool thread in Cherry (overdyed)
- Size 10 transparent Delica beads in Lilac
- C-Lon beading thread in Lilac
- DMC perle cotton #8 in black
- Milliners, chenille, embroidery, and beading needles

Prework

Refer to the placement guide patterns for the mat and the coasters (pages 71 and 72) and to Refresh Me (page 88) for detailed instructions.

1. Create clear vinyl placement guides.

2. Create tissue-paper embroidery guides.

3. Prepare the base fabric. (Do *not* cut apart if you are using the same piece of wool for both the mat and coasters.)

Construction

Refer to Refresh Me (page 88) for detailed instructions on freezer-paper patterns and the slanted-needle technique. Refer to Stitching Glossary (page 95) for an illustration of each stitch.

STEP ONE: PREPARING FOR APPLIQUÉ

Referring to the directions for the Wine Country appliquéd storage box top, prepare the wool appliqué leaves and berries, position and stitch the embroidery guide with green thread, and pin and baste the appliqué shapes in position.

STEPS TWO AND THREE: APPLIQUÉ, EMBROIDERY, AND BEADING

Referring to the directions for the *Wine Country* appliquéd box top:

1. Appliqué the leaves and berries to the mat and coasters.

2. Embroider the stems and veins.

3. Add transparent beads to the grapes on the serving mat as shown on the placement guide.

STEP FOUR: FINISHING

1. Place the completed appliqué pieces face-up on top of a piece of black wool. Pin in place.

2. Baste the outer edges at least ⅜″ from the white lines, using white cotton thread and a milliners needle.

3. Cut the front and back of each piece together, making sure to cut off the white lines.

4. Using a chenille needle and black perle cotton #8, blanket stitch the edges of the mat and coasters.

Wine Glass Charms

Finished leaf charm: 1½″ × 2″ • **Finished grape charm: 1″ × 1½″**

SUPPLIES

These supplies will make 4 charms, 2 in each style.

- Weeks Dye Works felted wool (*or* other wool fabric in similar colors):

  Collards (dark green): 2½″ × 4½″

  Meadow (light green): 2½″ × 6½″

  Bordeaux (dark magenta): 2½″ × 2½″

- Weeks Dye Works wool thread in Ivy (green, overdyed)

- Caron Impressions wool/silk thread in Cherry (overdyed)

- Valdani perle cotton #12 in Green Pastures 526 (green, overdyed)

- 10/0 transparent Delica beads in Lilac

- 10/0 transparent beads in Chartreuse

- C-Lon beading thread in Lilac and Chartreuse

- Milliners, chenille, embroidery, and beading needles

- Mini drill for making twisted cord

Construction

Refer to Refresh Me (page 88) for detailed instructions on freezer-paper patterns and the slanted-needle technique.
Refer to Stitching Glossary (page 95) for an illustration of each stitch.

STEP ONE: PREPARING FOR ASSEMBLY

1. Referring to the patterns (page 72), use freezer-paper methods to create the shapes for the leaves and grapes in 2 colors.

2. Put 2 leaves of the same color together and baste, making 2 leaves in Collards, 2 leaves in Meadow, 2 grape groupings in Bordeaux, and 2 grape groupings in Meadow.

3. Make 4 twisted cords 7½″ in length, using Valdani perle cotton. See Making Twisted Cord (page 87).
Start with 16 strands of perle cotton 24″ long.

STEP TWO: STITCHING THE ASSEMBLY

1. Blanket stitch the leaves together with the ends of the twisted cord tucked in between the 2 layers of each leaf. To do this, begin to the right of the center valley and blanket stitch the edges, stopping just to the left of the valley. Remove the basting thread and tuck the twisted cord end inside. Blanket stitch, catching the twisted cord. Wrap the thread around the twisted cord a few times to secure before burying the knot.

2. Blanket stitch the grapes, using the Cherry thread. Use tiny blind stitches to catch the twisted cord between the grapes just before you stitch the second grape to the first.

3. Embellish the veins on the leaves, using the Ivy thread.

4. Add beads to the grapes, using Lilac beads for the Bordeaux grapes and Chartreuse beads for the Meadow grapes.

Wine Bottle Snug

Finished size: 3½″ diameter × 6″

This wool snug will dress up any bottle for a beautiful gift, or look elegant on a bottle on your bar or buffet.

SUPPLIES

- Weeks Dye Works felted wool (*or* other wool fabric in similar colors):
  Bordeaux (dark magenta), 10″ × 12″ for base
  Collards (dark green), 10″ × 15″
  Meadow (light green), 2″ × 6″
- Caron Impressions wool/silk thread in Cherry (overdyed)
- Weeks Dye Works wool thread in Ivy (green, overdyed)
- Milliners, chenille, and embroidery needles

Prework

Refer to the placement guide patterns (pages 73 and 74) and to Refresh Me (page 88) for detailed instructions.

1. Create clear vinyl placement guides.

2. Create tissue-paper embroidery guides.

3. Prepare the base fabric for each of the 4 panels.

Construction

Refer to Refresh Me (page 88) for detailed instructions on freezer-paper patterns and the slanted-needle technique. Refer to Stitching Glossary (page 95) for an illustration of each stitch.

STEP ONE: PREPARING FOR APPLIQUÉ

1. Referring to the patterns (page 73), use freezer-paper methods to create the wool appliqué shapes.

2. Line up and hinge the placement guides at the top of each Merlot felted wool base, securing with 2 or 3 straight pins along the top edge.

3. Position the embroidery guides and pin in place. Remove the placement guides and stitch the embroidery guides, using green sewing thread.

4. Reposition and hinge the placement guide at the top of each wool base.

5. Place the appliqué shapes in position and pin.

6. Baste all shapes, using white cotton thread and a milliners needle.

STEP TWO: APPLIQUÉ AND EMBROIDERY

1. Appliqué the leaves with the Ivy thread, using the slanted needle technique.

2. Using the same thread, stem stitch the veins on the leaves and the curling vines.

STEP THREE: ASSEMBLY

1. Place the appliqué panels on the Collards felted wool lining and baste the entire perimeter of each panel.

2. Label the panels to keep them in order when assembling. Cut out the appliquéd panels and linings together.

3. Blanket stitch the entire perimeter of each panel, using the Cherry thread, burying the knots between the layers.

4. Line up the panels matching the bottom edges as indicated.

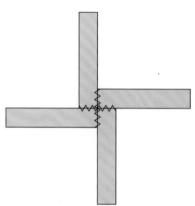

Wine snug assembly

5. Whipstitch the blanket-stitched edges from the center bottom to the top of each panel, using a matching sewing thread. Catch the blanket stitches but not the wool fabric in each stitch.

Add your favorite bottle of wine!

Wine Country Storage Box—top

Schematic diagram:
Wine Country Storage Box—top

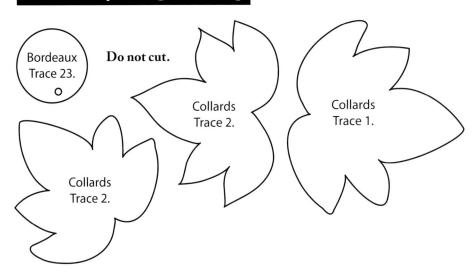

Bordeaux
Trace 23.

Do not cut.

Collards
Trace 2.

Collards
Trace 1.

Collards
Trace 2.

Wine Country Storage Box—side

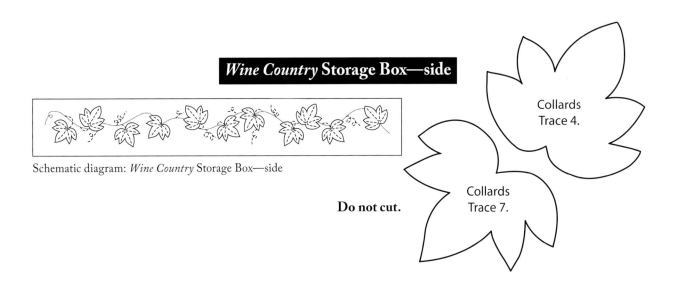

Schematic diagram: *Wine Country* Storage Box—side

Collards
Trace 4.

Collards
Trace 7.

Do not cut.

Wine Country Serving Mat

Collards
Trace 1.

Do not cut.

Bordeaux
Trace 13.

Collards
Trace 1.

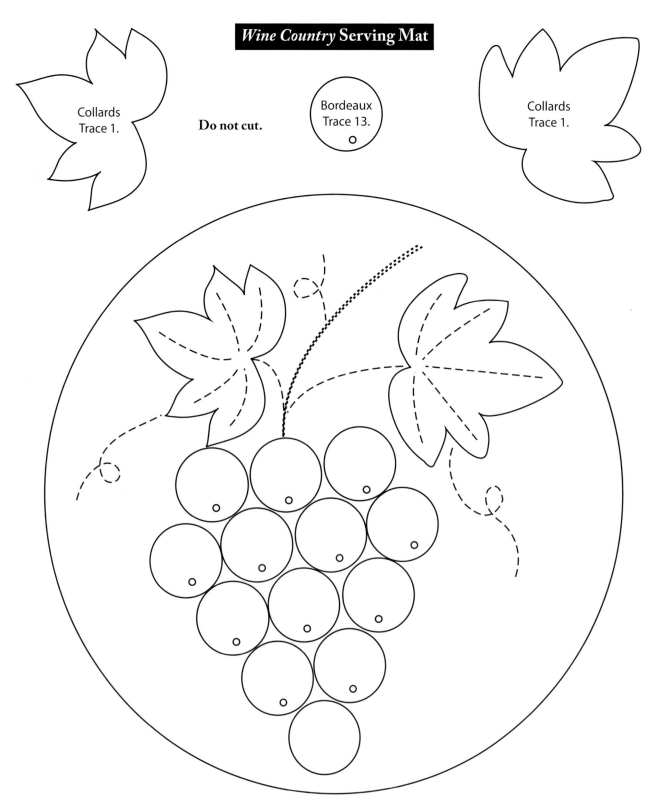

Placement guide pattern: *Wine Country* Serving Mat

Wine Country: Working with Embroidery Guides • 71

Wine Country Coasters

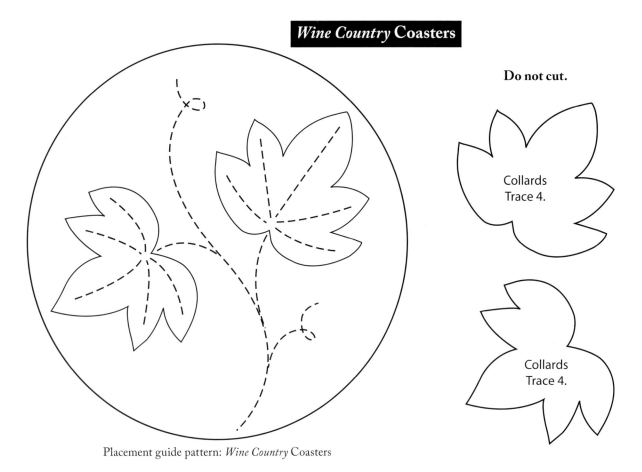

Do not cut.

Collards
Trace 4.

Collards
Trace 4.

Placement guide pattern: *Wine Country* Coasters

Wine Country Wine Glass Charms

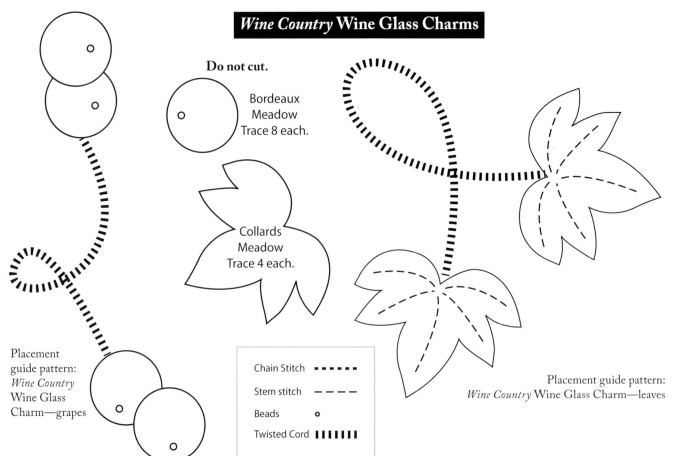

Do not cut.

Bordeaux
Meadow
Trace 8 each.

Collards
Meadow
Trace 4 each.

Placement
guide pattern:
Wine Country
Wine Glass
Charm—grapes

Chain Stitch	● ● ● ● ●
Stem stitch	– – – – –
Beads	o
Twisted Cord	I I I I I I I

Placement guide pattern:
Wine Country Wine Glass Charm—leaves

Wine Country **Wine Bottle Snug**

Placement guide patterns:
Wine Country Wine Bottle Snug—
panels 1 and 2

Stem Stitch ─ ─ ─ ─ ─ ─ ─

Do not cut.

Collards
Trace 5.
Meadow
Trace 3.

Panel 1

Panel 2

Placement guide patterns:
Wine Country Wine Bottle Snug—
panels 3 and 4

Panel 3

Panel 4

Happy Home:
A Lesson in Trapunto

Skill level: Confident beginner/intermediate

The Pennsylvania Hex sign for "happy home" includes hearts and tulips representing the love for home and family. The Pennsylvania Dutch people took great pride in both family and home with care and comfort being given to gardening. Tulips were brought from the Dutch countryside to remember the homeland.

This suite of bedroom accessories brings the traditions of the Pennsylvania Dutch to today's living with a pillow, candle mat and e-reader blanket. These three pieces look wonderfully cozy together appointing a bedroom.

Trapunto is the Italian word for quilting and has been come to describe a stuffing technique for quilting and appliqué. In this project the slanted-needle technique is critical to achieve the puff in the heart which can then be stuffed from the back.

Round Pillow

Finished size: 15″ diameter, plus 2″ ruffle

SUPPLIES

- White felted wool for base, 17″ × 17″

- Weeks Dye Works wool (*or* other wool fabric in similar colors):
  Merlot (deep red), 7″ × 10″
  Collards (dark green), 6″ × 6″
  Mustard (golden yellow), 6″ × 7″
  Louisiana Hot Sauce (dark red), 3½″ × 6″
  Meadow (light green), 2″ × 8″

- Weeks Dye Works wool thread in Saffron (light gold) and Cayenne (red)

- Bella Lusso wool thread in Pine 675 (green) and Chianti 576 (burgundy)

- Medici wool thread in Green 8342

- Milliners, chenille, and embroidery needles

- Cotton fabric, predominately burgundy with gold and or green accents, ¾ yard

- 10″ matching invisible zipper

- Round pillow form, 14″ diameter

- Polyester craft stuffing

Prework

Refer to the placement guide pattern (pullout page P2) and to Refresh Me (page 88) for detailed instructions.

1. Make a clear vinyl placement guide.

2. Prepare the base fabric.

Construction

Refer to Refresh Me (page 88) for detailed instructions on freezer-paper patterns and the slanted-needle technique. Refer to Stitching Glossary (page 95) for an illustration of each stitch.

STEP ONE: PREPARING FOR APPLIQUÉ

1. Referring to the patterns (page 82), use freezer-paper methods to create the wool appliqué shapes. Refer to the cutting tip for cutting accurate tulip shapes. Rough cut the pieces and then trim them individually for accuracy.

---

tip *For accuracy in cutting tulips follow the cutting guide. The first cut should stop at the center bottom. The second cut will end the same.*

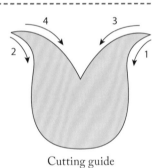

Cutting guide

---

2. Using rotary cutting tools, cut 4 narrow rectangles ¼˝ × 7½˝ of Meadow wool for the stems.

3. Line up and hinge the placement guide at the top of the felted wool base, securing with 3–5 straight pins along the top edge.

4. Place the appliqué shapes in position and pin, beginning with the stems. To preserve the stems, pin by taking a bite from either side of the base fabric, allowing the pin to anchor the stem without piercing it. This will keep the stems straight.

5. Baste all shapes, using white cotton thread and a milliners needle.

STEP TWO: APPLIQUÉ

1. Using a length of Genziana green wool thread and a chenille needle, herringbone stitch the stems in place. This decorative stitch will help keep the narrow stems in place without fraying and add interesting texture to the design.

2. Appliqué the center leaves with the burgundy wool thread, using the slanted-needle stitch.

3. Appliqué the tulips and tulip centers with matching threads, continuing to use the slanted-needle stitch.

4. Appliqué the hearts with burgundy thread and use an exaggerated slanted-needle stitch. This will make the hearts puff and leave the desired room for stuffing.

STEP THREE: TRAPUNTO

1. Working from the back, cut a 1½˝ opening in the base fabric behind an appliquéd heart.

2. Place a small amount of craft stuffing between the layers and move it around, using a wooden chopstick or other implement to evenly disperse.

3. Once you are pleased with the amount of puffiness added to the heart, close the opening in the back, using a whipstitch and white cotton thread. Repeat for all 4 hearts.

STEP FOUR: FINISHING

The pillow can be finished in a variety of methods. The sample features a 2˝ ruffle and a invisible zipper in the back so a 14˝ round pillow form can easily be inserted and removed.

Candle Mat

Finished size: 9˝ diameter

SUPPLIES

- White felted wool for base, 10˝ × 10˝

- Weeks Dye Works fabrics (*or other wool fabric in similar colors*):
  Merlot (deep red), 3˝ × 3½˝
  Collards (dark green), 12˝ × 12˝
  Mustard (golden yellow), 4½˝ × 4½˝
  Louisiana Hot Sauce (dark red), 3˝ × 4˝

- Weeks Dye Works wool threads in Saffron (light gold) and Cayenne (red)

- Bella Lusso wool thread in Pine 675 (green) and Chianti 576 (burgundy)

- Valdani perle cotton #12 in Green Pastures 526 (green, overdyed)

- Milliners, chenille, and embroidery needles

Prework

Refer to the placement guide pattern (page 83) and to Refresh Me (page 88) for detailed instructions.

1. Create a clear vinyl placement guide.

2. Create a tissue-paper embroidery guide.

3. Prepare the base fabric.

Construction

Refer to Refresh Me (page 88) for detailed instructions on freezer-paper patterns and the slanted-needle technique. Refer to Stitching Glossary (page 95) for an illustration of each stitch.

STEP ONE: PREPARING FOR APPLIQUÉ

1. Referring to the patterns (page 83), use freezer-paper methods to create the wool appliqué shapes.

2. Line up and hinge the placement guide at the top of the felted wool base, securing with 3–5 straight pins along the top edge.

3. Position the embroidery guide and pin in place. Remove the placement guide and stitch the embroidery guide, using green sewing thread.

4. Using Collards thread and a chenille needle, chainstitch the stems over the stitches made with the embroidery guide.

5. Reposition and hinge the placement guide at the top of the wool base.

6. Place the appliqué shapes in position and pin.

7. Baste all shapes, using white cotton thread and a milliners needle.

STEP TWO: APPLIQUÉ

Appliqué the leaves, tulips, hearts, and tulip centers in that order, using matching thread and the slanted-needle stitch. Follow these guidelines for increased accuracy:

- Make sure the center of the tulip is lined up with the valley of the scallop on all 4 sides.
- Make sure the hearts also are lined up with a scallop.
- Begin with the tulip tips on either side to make sure they remain even.

STEP THREE: FINISHING

Refer to Finishing a Candle Mat (page 87) for detailed instructions.

1. Cut out the scalloped edge of the candle mat. Snip the valleys after cutting to sharpen them.

2. Use a piece of Collards wool for the mat backing and Valdani perle cotton in Green Pastures for blanket stitching.

E-Reader Blanket

Finished size: 5½″ × 8″ closed

This charming blanket is perfect for storing your e-reader on the night stand or side table. The directions here are for a blanket, but you can easily stitch the sides if you prefer to have a pocket. This E-Reader Blanket was made to fit a Kindle Fire. Measure your e-reader and adjust the pattern to fit.

SUPPLIES

- White felted wool for base, 14″ × 9″

- Weeks Dye Works wool (*or other wool fabric in similar colors*):

  Collards (dark green), 9″ × 15″

  Mustard (golden yellow), 4½″ × 4½″

  Louisiana Hot Sauce (dark red), 3″ × 4″

- Weeks Dye Works wool threads in Saffron (light gold) and Cayenne (red)

- Bella Lusso wool thread in Pine 675 (green)

- Valdani perle cotton #12 in Green Pastures 526 (green, overdyed)

- Milliners, chenille, and embroidery needles

- Skirtex (upholstery stabilizer)

- Hook-and-loop circles, ⅜″ white

Prework

Refer to the placement guide pattern (pullout page P2) and to Refresh Me (page 88) for detailed instructions.

1. Create a clear vinyl placement guide.

2. Create a tissue-paper embroidery guide.

3. Prepare the base fabric (be sure to include the shapes for the tulips). Measure your e-reader and adjust the measurements in the following diagram to fit. Not including the silhouette for the tulips, the rectangle for the sample e-reader blanket measures 11″ × 8″. Use the placement guide pattern to create the left edge of the guide, including the cut edge of the tulips, then measure with rotary tools to extend the markings for the remainder of the rectangle.

Construction

Refer to Refresh Me (page 88) for detailed instructions on freezer-paper patterns and the slanted-needle technique. Refer to Stitching Glossary (page 95) for an illustration of each stitch.

STEP ONE: PREPARING FOR APPLIQUÉ

1. Referring to the patterns (page 82), use freezer-paper methods to create the wool appliqué shapes. Follow the cutting diagram for tulips (page 77).

2. Line up and hinge the placement guide at the top of the felted wool base, securing with 3–5 straight pins along the top edge.

3. Position the embroidery guide and pin in place. Remove the placement guide and stitch the embroidery guide, using green sewing thread.

4. Using a chenille needle and a single length of Collards thread, chainstitch the stems over the stitches made with the embroidery guide.

5. Reposition and hinge the placement guide at the top of the wool base.

6. Place the appliqué shapes in position and pin.

7. Baste all shapes, using white cotton thread and a milliners needle.

STEP TWO: APPLIQUÉ

Using a chenille needle and matching threads, appliqué the tulips, the tulip centers, and then the leaves, using the slanted-needle technique.

STEP THREE: FINISHING

The stabilizer is cut into sections to avoid stabilizer in the folds which would make the blanket difficult to fold. The design allows for stabilizer in the flaps, spine, and back. You may need to adjust the measurements slightly to fit your e-reader.

1. Cut the Skirtex stabilizer as follows:

- 1 rectangle 3˝ × 7½˝ for the left flap
- 1 rectangle 3¼˝ × 7½˝ for the right flap (behind the tulips)
- 2 rectangles ½˝ × 7½˝ for the spines
- 1 rectangle 4˝ × 7½˝ for the back

2. Cut out the completed appliqué, using rotary tools for 3 edges and scissors for the edge with the tulips.

3. Place the stabilizer pieces on the back of the appliquéd base in the following order: 3¼˝ piece, ½˝ piece, 4˝ piece, ½˝ piece, and 3˝ piece. Pin and baste.

4. Place the appliquéd base piece onto the Collards backing rectangle wrong sides together and fold around your e-reader for placement. Baste, keeping the blanket folded slightly at both edges.

5. Cut out the backing fabric, aligning it carefully with the front appliqué and folding the entire blanket as you fit the backing. Cut it straight behind the tulips. Ultimately, the lining will need to be slightly smaller than the outside for the blanket to fold without interior wrinkles. When opened, it will not lie perfectly flat.

6. Blanket stitch the perimeter, using Valdani perle cotton, skipping the area behind the tulips.

7. Add a hook-and-loop tape closure behind each tulip. Strengthen with sewing thread around the edges.

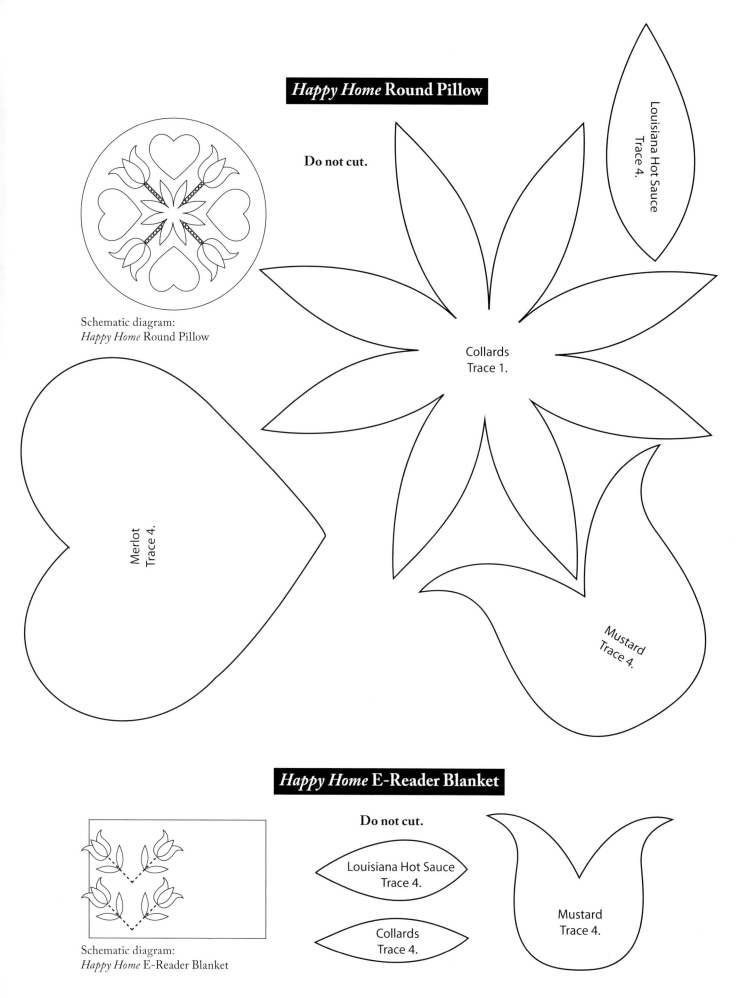

Happy Home Round Pillow

Schematic diagram:
Happy Home Round Pillow

Do not cut.

Louisiana Hot Sauce
Trace 4.

Collards
Trace 1.

Merlot
Trace 4.

Mustard
Trace 4.

Happy Home E-Reader Blanket

Schematic diagram:
Happy Home E-Reader Blanket

Do not cut.

Louisiana Hot Sauce
Trace 4.

Collards
Trace 4.

Mustard
Trace 4.

Happy Home Candle Mat

Schematic diagram:
Happy Home Candle Mat

Do not cut.

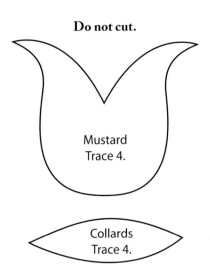

Mustard
Trace 4.

Collards
Trace 4.

Louisiana Hot Sauce
Trace 4.

Merlot
Trace 4.

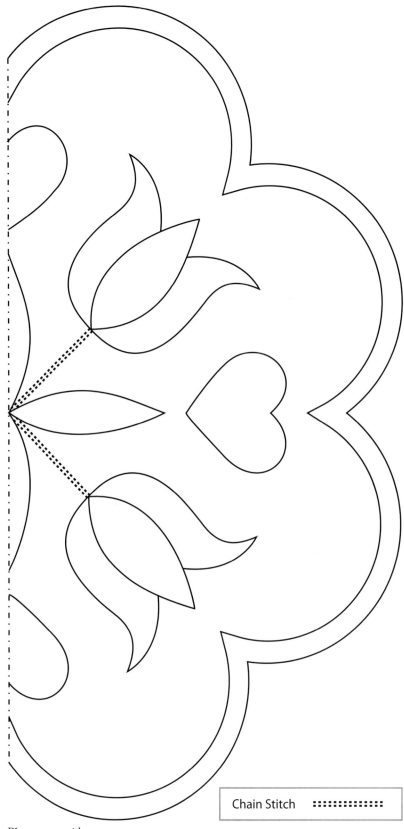

| Chain Stitch | :::::::::::: |

Placement guide pattern:
Happy Home Candle Mat

Making Covered Boxes

Covered boxes are fun to make and the possibilities are endless. Choose fabrics, ornaments, and appliqué designs and create covered boxes in your own personal style. Craft stores carry a wide range of boxes from round to rectangular and even heart-shaped.

The lids can be a single color, or circular boxes can be one color for the top and a complementing color for the lid side. Trims, beads, buttons, and appliqué designs can be blended for unique looks in accessory boxes, jewelry boxes, and gift boxes. Have fun designing and covering your own boxes.

COVERING A ROUND BOX

Before covering the box with wool, measure it for the lining pieces. Measure the depth and circumference of the outside and trace the bottom.

Box Lid

The lid is constructed by covering a cardboard disk the same size as the top of the box and sewing it to the lid side which is covered with wool. The top is also lined with batting to give the lid puff and stature.

1. Cut 2 pieces of batting, one the exact size of the live appliqué area and one the size of the pattern cutting line.

2. Cut out the appliqué top along the cutting line, leaving the running stitch guide in place for the live area. This will help you position the top piece accurately. The cutting line should be at least 1¼″ larger than the live appliqué area.

3. Cut a piece of stiff cardboard the size of the box lid. (It may be necessary to use 3 pieces of cardboard stapled together to achieve the appropriate amount of stiffness if you use a shirt gift box or something of similar weight).

4. Sandwich as follows:

• Appliquéd top (face down) on the bottom

• Large circular piece of batting

• Smaller piece of batting for additional puff

• Circular cardboard assembly on the top

5. Using white quilting thread doubled, stitch running stitches around the edge of the appliquéd top and batting and gather the entire piece over the circular cardboard. Pull the running stitches tightly to gather the batting appliqué assembly around the cardboard and secure with additional stitches. Secure as tightly as possible with a double knot.

Covering the Lid Side

1. Using rotary cutting methods, cut a piece of felted wool the size of the lid side plus ¾″ by the circumference of the lid plus ½″.

2. Using Elmer's school glue and a 1″ paintbrush, carefully paint the side and ¾″ around the top of the lid with a layer of glue.

3. Press the lid piece along the side flush with the bottom of the lid and over onto the lid top, cutting small V's out of the felted wool along the edge.

The felted wool will easily mold to the box lid but the extra fabric will need to be eliminated on top by cutting out these tiny areas.

4. Where the edges meet, cut a tiny bit off to butt the two sides together closely. Glue the sides first and then move to the top, cutting the V's as you glue down the fabric and press smooth.

- -

tips for Gluing Wool to Boxes

• *Put the glue in a small container just large enough to dip the paintbrush in.*

• *Prepare the glue and the paintbrush so when you are ready to glue these items are ready to go.*

• *Work quickly when applying glue and spread it in a smooth layer across the papier-mâché surface.*

• *Clean the paintbrush immediately in hot water so the glue does not harden and ruin the paintbrush.*

• *Be careful not to get glue on the wool; it's difficult to remove. If you do, try to remove it immediately with warm water and a rag.*

- -

Box Side

1. With the lid on the box, use a pencil to mark the bottom of the lid on the box side. This will be where the felted wool side covering will begin. Since felted wool is so thick and fluffy, it is not advisable to cover the part of the box side covered by the lid.

2. Cut a piece of felted wool the size of the marked side plus ¾" by the circumference of the side plus ½".

3. Paint the side and bottom of the box with glue as done with the lid top and press the felted wool onto the side and bottom. As with the lid top, cut away small V's on the bottom to prevent fabric from bunching.

Let these pieces dry overnight.

Lid Assembly

Once the lid side is completely dry, you can sew the lid top to it. Using a double length of matching quilting thread with a knot at the end, sew the lid top to the lid side, using the ladder stitch. Every 5 or 6 stitches, pull the thread tight before continuing. Bury the knots inside when completed.

Lining

1. Using the measurements taken before covering the box, cut pieces of felted wool. Trim the pieces to fit the inside of the box. The pieces should be flush against each other without any overlap.

2. Glue to the box following Tips for Gluing Wool to Boxes (page 85).

COVERING A SQUARE BOX

All the box patterns in this book are for round boxes. But some appliqué patterns, such as *Holiday Laurel* (page 41), lend themselves beautifully for use on a square box lid.

Box Lid

Covering a square box does not require a separate lid side piece. The top and lid side can be covered with batting and the edges mitered for a sharp look. Decorative trim is always an excellent idea for a professional finish.

1. Cut a piece of batting the exact size of the box top for a little padding.

2. Cut the completed appliquéd top with enough room for the box lid sides on all 4 sides. These can be trimmed flush with the box top later.

3. Using Elmer's school glue and a 1" paintbrush, carefully paint the box top with a thin layer of glue.

4. Apply the batting squarely to the box top and press to adhere.

5. Position the prepared appliquéd piece to the top of the box, lining up the outline of the base shape.

6. Paint each lid side with glue and press the side piece down, allowing the corners to fold outwards. Work opposite sides first and allow the glue to dry before trimming.

7. Clip the corners flush with the side up to the top of the corner and butt the wool together.

8. Let the corners dry completely.

9. Trim the bottom of the lid sides with scissors or a very sharp rotary cutter.

10. Add decorative trim for a professional finish.

Box Side

1. With the lid on the box, use a pencil to mark the bottom of the lid onto the box side. This will be where the felted wool appliqué side covering will begin. Since felted wool is so thick and fluffy it is not advisable to cover the part of the box covered by the lid.

2. Cut a piece of felted wool the size of the marked side plus ¾″ by the perimeter of the box plus ½″.

3. Paint the side and bottom of the box with glue as done with the lid top and press the felted wool onto the sides, smoothing over the corners.

4. Cut away small V's on the bottom corners to miter neatly and prevent the fabric from bunching.

Finishing a Candle Mat

1. Place the completed appliquéd base piece face-up on top of a piece of wool, making sure you have enough room on the outside edge for a ⅜″ border. Pin in place.

2. Using a milliners needle and basting thread, baste around the entire perimeter of the piece, keeping the basting stitches at least ⅜″ from the edge.

3. Using a chenille needle and matching thread, blanket stitch the edge of the appliquéd base piece to the backing.

4. Trim the backing to leave a ⅜″ border. For increased accuracy, add a dotted line using a Micron pen and a ruler all the way around before cutting.

Making Twisted Cord

1. The general rule for making twisted cord is to cut the threads to be used 3 times longer than the finished cord. On each, tie one end in a knot. Tie the other end with 2 knots, one at the end and another ½″ in.

2. Place the hook of the mini drill between the two knots on one end. Secure the other end or let a friend hold it. Begin cranking to twist the thread. When the thread begins to kink, it is ready to be folded in half and twist itself together. Holding both ends, gently remove the mini drill and add it to the center of the cord, allowing the weight of the mini drill to fold it in half and twist together. The end can be knotted, then glued so it will stay after the knots are cut away. Let the glue rest overnight.

Refresh Me

Tools and Supplies

NEEDLES

Use milliners or straw needles when basting or stitching through embroidery guides. Use chenille needles to appliqué the felted wool pieces. I prefer size 24. My favorite size of embroidery needle is 4.

TWEEZERS

This is a critical tool for placing shapes under a placement guide. Locking tweezers are best for they eliminate hand tension.

VINYL

For placement guides, use a transparent material such as 8 mm vinyl, which is available on the bolt at fabric stores. Mark with a Sharpie marker in fine, not ultra-fine.

TISSUE PAPER

For marking embroidery lines, use white tissue paper sold for gift wrapping. This is available in most stores that carry wrapping paper.

Locking tweezers

SCISSORS

Use scissors with short blades and large handles when cutting out small shapes.

GLUE

A little fabric glue holds tiny pieces in place. Be careful not to use too much and to keep glue away from the areas you will needle. It's not easy to move a needle through glue-soaked wool fabric.

THREAD

Wool

Wool thread is my choice for felted wool appliqué because it is organic, literally disappears if matched correctly with appliqué pieces, and easily sails through felted wool. It makes sewing a pleasure. There are many different types that come on spools and in skeins.

Wool thread is made from lamb's wool, merino, or alpaca. Lamb's wool is the softest and easiest to work with. Merino and alpaca have more drag and are often sticky when sewing through wool fabric.

Wool thread is often used in crewel embroidery and is sometimes referred to as *crewel thread*. Crewel refers to the weight. Tapestry thread is also made with wool but is twice as thick as crewel weight. Threads range in weight from two-ply lace-weight yarn to a very fine wool thread found on a spool.

Wool thread is often found in embroidery, needlepoint, and online shops and does not need to be split but is always used as is. Some manufacturers create wool/silk blends, which have added sheen.

Floss

Cotton floss comes in six-stranded skeins and is generally separated into strands (called stripping) to allow the stitcher to decide how thick the embroidery should be. In the majority of the designs in this book, floss is used in a single strand and is therefore split.

Silk floss often comes in twelve-stranded skeins and is generally much more expensive than cotton floss. Silk creates more of a shine; I avoid using it unless I want a shiny look to my embroidery.

Perle

Perle cotton is a single-stranded cotton thread that is available in three weights: #5, #8, and #12, with the latter being the thinnest. Perle cotton is found in skeins or wrapped balls and is often used for decorative embellishments, blanket-stitched edges, and twisted cord.

Felted Wool

The projects in this book are made from felted wool, which is wool fabric that has been felted (shrunk) to avoid fray. I like how it looks, feels, and sews. Note that it is not the same thing as wool felt.

Felted wool is woven wool yardage that has a weft and a warp. When this yardage is felted, it is shrunk in hot water, followed by high-heat drying, causing it to constrict and become dense. This fabric is easy to needle because the holes between the warp and weft remain. Once felted, woven wool yardage will not easily fray.

On the other hand, wool felt is made from wool roving that is pressed into sheets, using hot water and high heat, causing it to become dense. This fabric is slightly more difficult to needle because it has no holes as in a woven fabric.

Some wool felt is a blend of 70% wool and 30% polyester and performs well in a variety of applications because it has absolutely no fray. For very tiny pieces, or if I need a specific color that I am unable to find or dye in felted wool, I will use wool felt.

Craft felt is made from 100% synthetic materials, and some is even made using recycled plastic bottles. It feels and performs very differently from wool. This material should not be used with freezer-paper patterns, because the ironing will cause the paper to permanently bond with the fabric.

Melton wool is not felted, but it, too, is an excellent choice for appliqué. Melton is a heavy cloth that is tightly woven and finished with a smooth face, concealing the weave. It is often used for overcoats.

FELTING YOUR OWN WOOL

Felting wool is a great way to add unique elements to your projects. Wool yardage is easily transformed into felt with a home washing machine. Experiment with a bit of felting, to see how beautifully these natural fibers behave as you sculpt your creations.

It's easy to felt wool at home. With the right wool fabric, or even old sweaters and other clothes, you can make felted wool! Choose fabrics that are 100% wool. But stay away from gabardine, because it has many more warp yarns than weft ones and does not felt evenly.

Wash your wool yardage in hot water with a little detergent; then tumble dry at high heat. The fabric will shrink nicely. The longer you dry it, the more it will shrink and felt, becoming denser. Check its progress.

Agitation in the washer positively affects the felting process. The old top loaders were the best in terms of agitation, but my front loader works fine. Remove the wool from the dryer as soon as the cycle is complete to avoid wrinkles.

Occasionally you might find a piece of felted wool fabric in a shop that almost seems as though it has not been felted. The maker may have dye-processed and felted the fabric in one step. With less agitation, this fabric is less felted—it won't be as thick or fully felted.

Prework

The key to making an appliqué project go smoothly is to take the time to make accurate tracings for the patterns and to create placement and embroidery guides. While not necessarily fun, this work is critical for accurately placed appliqué pieces and stitches. The payoff comes when you have a clearly defined place for your shapes and you can chain stitch to your heart's content, following a running stitch guide that clearly marks your path.

PREPARE THE BASE FABRIC

A white stitched line shows the live appliqué area for the *Tesoritos* Mini Treasure Box top (page 23).

Whatever the final shape of your project—whether square, circle, or oval—it is important to mark the edges in order to center the appliqué design accurately. When making a pattern for the base for wool projects, use a freezer-paper pattern and a pen.

1. Trace the pattern for the project base onto the matte side of a piece of freezer paper. Some of the symmetrical designs are shown as partial patterns; rotate the freezer paper to trace the whole pattern. Base pieces that are squares or rectangles can be measured and then cut with rotary tools.

2. Cut out the shape and iron it onto your wool fabric with a hot iron. The shiny side of the freezer paper should against the fabric. For projects with multiple base pieces, the freezer-paper patterns can be ironed to one larger piece of wool instead of smaller, individual pieces.

3. Trace a line around the outside of the freezer-paper pattern onto the wool fabric. Use a white gel pen if the fabric is dark or a black fine archival pen if the fabric is light. Keep the pen completely perpendicular to the fabric so that the ink flows easily and your marks are smooth.

4. Remove the freezer paper. You will have a line marking the edge of the design area, which can be cut away once the appliqué and embroidery are completed. Do not cut out the base fabric shape until you are finished with your appliqué and embroidery; the base and the backing should always be cut together.

5. Rough cut around the shape so that there will be less fabric to deal with as you work. For the base shape, cut about ½″ larger than the marked line all the way around; for especially small shapes, cut ¼″ larger.

6. For some projects, such as a covered box lid, you will need to mark the live appliqué area on the base. Make a freezer-paper pattern of the live appliqué area, shown with dashed lines on the placement guide. Adhere to the back of the base fabric and trace. Using a milliners needle and white cotton thread, stitch small running stitches on the white line completely around the circle, making sure your needle goes all the way through the black felted wool. Flip the piece over and you should have a white stitching line as your guide for the live area for appliqué.

MAKE A PLACEMENT GUIDE

1. Position a piece of clear plastic acetate or vinyl over the pattern and tape it in place to avoid slippage.

2. Use a fine permanent marker (not ultra-fine) to trace the lines of the design with as much detail as possible. Make sure to trace the outer shape of the item so you will be able to position the design accurately on your base fabric. Some of the symmetrical designs are shown as partial patterns; rotate the acetate or vinyl to trace the whole design.

3. The placement guide is hinged to the base fabric with straight pins. This will allow you to flip the guide up and down to position the pieces underneath and in their proper place.

---

tip *Write your name on the right side of the guide so you will not inadvertently use it upside down. (Trust me, it's easy to make that mistake!)*

MAKE AN EMBROIDERY GUIDE

Embroidery is most enjoyable when the stitcher knows exactly where to place the needle next. Embroidery guides enable the maker to develop rhythm and to focus on even stitches. They are especially helpful when a design includes curling vines and stems.

1. Position a piece of tissue paper over the placement guide and use a pencil to trace all the lines that will be embroidered. Indicate the outside shape of the item, too (be it a table mat, pillow, or pincushion), so that you will be able to position the guide correctly onto the base fabric. Indicate where the top, bottom, right, and left sides are. Trace the outlines of other shapes to aid in placing the guide correctly later.

2. Mark the right side of your tissue by writing your name.

3. Separate the tissue paper from the original pattern and retrace the pencil lines with a marker so you have clear marks to use when placing the tissue onto the felted wool base.

Tips for Stitching Through Tissue Paper

- Make sure your pins are 3″ apart to prevent slippage while stitching in-hand.

- Use a thin, long needle such as a milliners or straw needle.

- The thread length should amount to fewer than two lengths from your fingertips to the crease in your elbow.

- Use a backstitch at the beginning and the end of each line. Do not use knots.

- Try to fill the needle with at least 3 stitches before drawing the thread through.

- Every few stitches, you can roll the needle toward you to uncurl the thread; this will prevent knots.

- If your thread knots, slip your needle inside the loop of the knot and pull to the right to unknot.

- Manipulate and move the fabric between your fingers to make the stitching easier.

4. Position the marked tissue-paper guide on the base fabric, aligning the marked outer lines on the guide and the base fabric. For additional help in correct placement, you can hinge the placement guide on the base first, position the marked tissue-paper guide, then remove the placement guide for now. Pin the tissue embroidery guide in place, avoiding the traced lines to be embroidered.

5. Using cotton thread that matches the color of the thread you will use to embroider, stitch running stitches, as tiny as possible, through the lines onto the wool base. (You will ultimately embroider over these lines with wool thread, covering them.) Begin and end with a backstitch, leaving a tail of approximately 1″ at either end.

6. Rip the tissue away in quick motions toward the stitched line. Use tweezers to remove any residual tissue from the stitches. If there are any loops in the lines of stitching, pull on the tails at either end to smooth them. Stretching the wool in both directions will also generally smooth out any loops. For stubborn loops, just pull them smooth from the back.

7. When you are satisfied with the stitching, cut the tails at either end flush with the wool base. You are now ready to embroider over the guiding stitches.

Freezer-Paper Patterns

1. Trace pattern pieces for sections or elements as you go. If you make too many at once, you are likely to lose the small pieces. (Trust me, you won't find them later on your elbow or on the dog!)

2. Trace pattern pieces onto the matte side of a piece of freezer paper. Iron the freezer-paper patterns, shiny side down, onto your felted wool fabric, grouping pattern pieces of the same color. If the fabric you are using is a small piece, create a cutting pattern, tracing all the pieces required for that particular color to make sure everything fits before cutting.

3. Rough cut the freezer-paper patterns by color for each piece, trimming close to—but not on—the cutting line so you can trim each piece separately. This will make cutting more accurate, as you will not have the weight of the fabric pulling as you cut.

4. Trim each shape with a sharp pair of scissors, using the freezer-paper tracing line as your guide. Do *not* remove the freezer paper. You may wish to write on the pieces to key them to your pattern and avoid confusion later.

Cutting Tools and Tips

- When cutting pieces smaller than 4″, a short blade is recommended. Use scissors with less than a 2″ blade and large comfortable handles, which makes cutting comfortable and easy.

- When cutting small pieces, make sure the scissors maintain contact with the fabric. As the scissors draw open, move the fabric into the blades maintaining contact with the fabric; this prevents the "jaggies." Cut with your dominant hand and rotate the fabric piece with your opposite hand.

- When cutting tiny pieces, follow these steps:

1. Cut the overall shape, leaving any smaller indented cuts untouched.

2. Change to embroidery scissors, preferably with a serrated edge, and cut these indents separately.

3. Press the pieces with the iron again if the freezer paper begins to pull away.

4. Overcut the corners if necessary, so the piece being cut will easily separate.

Basting the Pieces

1. Use while cotton thread and a milliners or straw needle to baste the appliqué pieces in position on the felted wool base.

2. Don't knot the thread; just double the first and last basting stitch instead.

3. Make straight stitches, which ultimately makes the basting stitches slant. This makes it easy to get embroidery scissors underneath and snip, easily pulling away the basting threads after the appliqué is completed.

Appliquéing with Felted Wool

Appliquéing with felted wool is different from appliquéing with traditional fabric. Draw your needle up from the base near the edge of your felted wool shape and place the down stitch directly opposite from where you came up. The stitches will show, so careful placement is critical. Use matching thread to make the stitch disappear as much as possible. Use wool thread to ensure that the thread will intertwine with the fabric.

For best results, use a light hand and a stab-stitch motion to appliqué wool. With a stab stitch, your stitches will be accurately placed, and carefully working around frayed threads is easier. Pull the thread gently, allowing a small loop of thread to rest lightly on the side of the appliqué piece. Complete the stitch without pulling tightly to avoid bunched edges.

Tips for Success in Felted Wool Appliqué

- Begin with a knot and end by taking your needle through 3 or 4 stitches and clip. Fewer knots on the back will reduce the chance of your needle inadvertently piercing a knot when embroidering.

- Use a thread no longer than 18″ and when threaded, no longer than the distance from your fingertips to your elbow.

- Move the thread along the needle often so it does not weaken at the needle hole and break.

- Keep your hand light, allowing the thread to gently rest on the edge of the appliqué piece.

- If a stitch seems too loose, tighten it after drawing the needle to the front as there will be more draw and more control.

tip *Wool thread and wool fabric have surface fibers that naturally intertwine. Use them together and your appliqué pieces will stay put.*

MOVING THE WORK

Keep the edge being appliquéd at the top when sewing; turning as needed. Rotating the appliqué keeps the edge being worked accessible and forcibly releases the tension in both the holding and working hands.

ADDING DIMENSION

Adding dimension to appliqué adds interest and creates excitement, especially when properly lit. Side lighting is the best way to show off dimensionality in felted wool appliqué pieces. A variety of methods can be used to add dimension, including trapunto, layering, and needle slanting.

Trapunto

Trapunto is a method of quilting with padded layers, producing a puffy, decorative look. Sometimes called the "stuffed technique," trapunto uses at least two layers, the underside of which is slit and padded, resulting in a raised surface on the quilt. This technique works especially well with fruit designs. The hearts in *Happy Home* (page 75) are a perfect example of the trapunto technique.

Layering

Layering pieces of felted wool also creates a dimensional effect. This technique makes the birds in *Love Birds* (page 51) appear sculpted and realistic.

Needle Slanting

Needle slanting is a technique for wool appliqué that was used for all the pieces in this book. By bringing up your needle at an angle just shy of the edge and then bringing it down at the same angle, the appliqué piece will be forced into a slight puff.

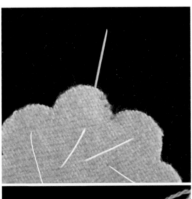

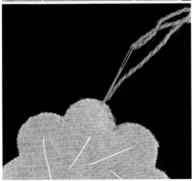

For the best effect, use a light hand—don't slant the stitches too much or you will get a puckered edge. Turn the work often so that each edge to be appliquéd is positioned to be easily stitched from right to left. (If you are left-handed, stitch from left to right.)

GETTING TO THE "POINT"

I am often asked what I do when I come to the point of an appliqué piece. The simple answer is to ignore it. When you come to a point, stitch on one side of it and then the other. Never stitch into the tip of a point; if you do, you will encourage fraying, and the point will not remain clean and sharp.

Guidelines for Embroidering over Running Stitches

Use a length of thread that is less than twice the length from your fingertips to your elbow crease. Wool thread is stressed when it is run through wool fabric, so shorter threads that change position on the needle as you sew will work best.

The rule of thumb when covering basting stitches with a stem stitch is to enter the fabric slightly to the left of the guide stitch and exit slightly to the right.

Stitching Glossary

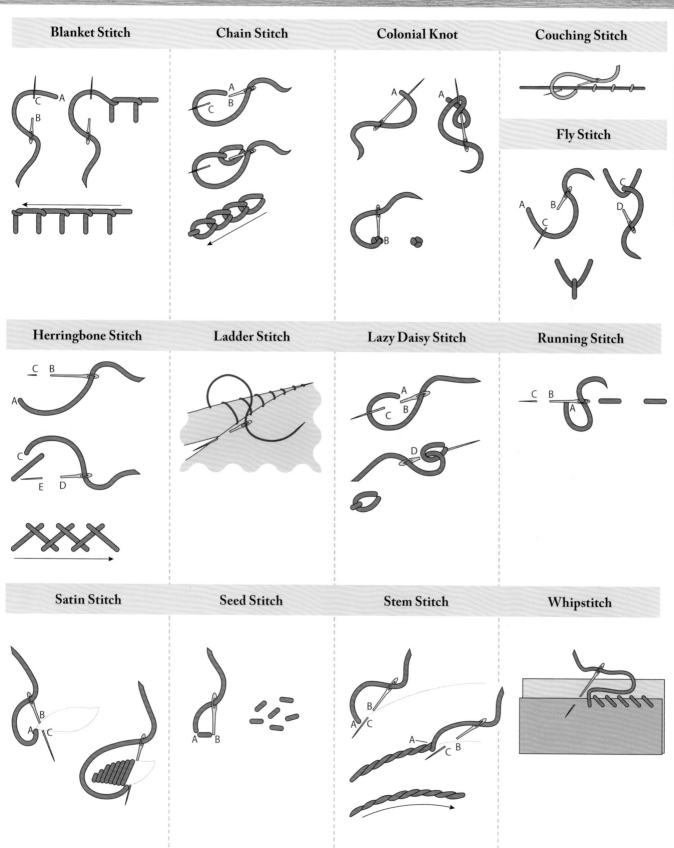

Blanket Stitch

Chain Stitch

Colonial Knot

Couching Stitch

Fly Stitch

Herringbone Stitch

Ladder Stitch

Lazy Daisy Stitch

Running Stitch

Satin Stitch

Seed Stitch

Stem Stitch

Whipstitch

About the Author

Photo by Julya Generoso

DEBORAH GALE TIRICO is an avid needle artist, designer, instructor, and author. She has studied appliqué with a variety of prominent teachers and continues to study historical appliqué quilts and coverlets.

Her specialty is the creation of a sculptural look to felted wool appliqué by using needle-slanting techniques and the layering and stuffing of wool pieces. Deborah's designs feature matching and overdyed wool threads and embroidery embellishments, which enhance and define the clarity of her subjects.

She is the author of two other books, *Gorgeous Wool Appliqué* and *A New Dimension in Wool Appliqué—Baltimore Album Style*, by C&T Publishing.

Also by Deborah Gale Tirico:

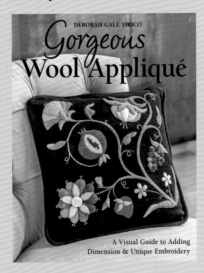

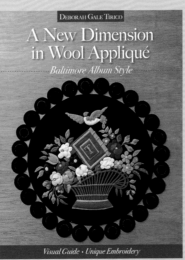

Visit Deborah online!

Website: deborahtirico.com